MAKING AND USING FINGER PUPPETS

MARGARET HUTCHINGS

with illustrations by
the author

photography by Eve Legg

MILLS & BOON LIMITED
LONDON

TAPLINGER
PUBLISHING COMPANY
NEW YORK

Other books by the same author

The 'What Shall I Do?' series
Toying with Trifles
Making Old Testament Toys
Making New Testament Toys
Modern Soft Toy Making
The Book of the Teddy Bear
Dolls and How to Make Them
Toys from the Tales of Beatrix
    Potter

First published in Great Britain in 1973 by
Mills & Boon Limited, 17–19 Foley Street,
London W1A IDR

First published in the United States in 1973 by
Taplinger Publishing Co, Inc, New York, New
York

British ISBN 0 263.05422 5

American ISBN 0–8008–5071–8

Library of Congress Catalog Card Number
73–814

Made and printed in Great Britain by
Morrison and Gibb Ltd, London and Edinburgh

Contents

4

Note to American Readers

The following terms may be
unfamiliar to American readers
and are accordingly clarified to
facilitate the use of this book.

knitting needles—British size 12
  equals American size 1; British
  size 10 equals American size 3
double yarn is comparable to sport
  yarn
bass—a woody fiber used to make
  cord or rope
beaker—a large wide-mouthed
  drinking cup
bobble—tassel, fringe or pom-pon
  trimming
bodkin—a large-eyed blunt-edge
  needle for drawing ribbon or tape
broderie anglaise—edging ribbon
  with open embroidery
busby—a headdress worn in the
  British army
mob cap—a woman's cap with a
  full crown and frills, fastened
  under chin
clothes peg—clothes pin
Copydex—adhesive, similar to
  Elmer's glue-all
diamanté—rhinestone
plait—braid
scrim—coarse cotton or linen fabric
  used for embroidery
stranded cotton—embroidery cotton
snippets—small pieces
Velcro—a self-adhering fabric used
  for fastening
Vilene—interlining, as pellon
wattle—fleshy and wrinkled skin
  hanging from chin or throat of
  rooster
$\frac{1}{2}$p piece—size of a nickel

Acknowledgements

The sweater on page 63 was
designed by my daughter-in-law,
Helen Hutchings.

The felt mice on page 80 were
designed by Dorothy Green and the
bears adapted by her from one of
my patterns.

The rhyme *Our Fat Black Cat* on
page 14 appears in *Playschool Play
Ideas* by Ruth Craft (BBC
Publications).

I am grateful to all the above for
their kind help and co-operation.

To Amanda, whom I hardly know,
but who obligingly started all this
by having her adenoids removed
at the crucial moment!

Foreword

A small boy was once asked to describe a Grandmother. 'They wear glasses', he said 'and funny underwear. They don't have anything to do except just be at home. Everybody should try to have one especially if they don't have television because Grannies are the only grown-ups who have got time to play.'

I am now the grandmother of two enchanting little girls—I do wear glasses, I don't wear funny underwear, I do have plenty to do except just being at home but I always have time to play and finger puppets, tremendous favourites with both Emma and Katie, figure prominently in that play.

The secret of success with these tiny puppets is that they must *fit*—gripping fingers of almost any size firmly and comfortably so as to avoid that insecure, slipping sensation. After all, what could be worse than to have the chief character take a sudden and unexpected dive to the floor right in the middle of a show or game? With this in mind the designs in this book have been carefully worked out to fit fingers of almost any size. The knitted puppets grip beautifully with no help at all and three sizes are given. Other types are held in place with thimbles, pipe cleaners or elastic, and having made one or two it will be easy to understand how sizes, types and colours can be interchanged and mixed at will.

This book is offered to all the family, to young and old, large and small, teachers and pupils, knitters, sewers and even 'stickers'. Everyone who enjoys making and doing should find scope for their talents. 'Makers' and 'doers' have piece drawers and every piece drawer contains many things which can usefully be turned into such tiny toys at almost no cost. Three inches of lace, two square inches of felt, six yards of knitting wool—of such are these characters built. For this reason I have not always given a 'materials list', particularly where it seems obvious that the worker will look at the picture in question and substitute some of my own suggestions for what she has by her. The usefulness of a finger puppet knows no bounds, indeed every mother who spends an evening making a secret hoard will bless the day she did so. One to slip into a pocket during moments of stress—that first day at school or a visit to the dentist, two to send as a gift to the small hostess of a birthday party, three to mount on a Christmas card, a series to produce at daily intervals during hospitalization (a special section appears about this!). The younger generation will enjoy making their own or sets for smaller brothers and sisters, and as teaching aids or 'attention holders' in school, these small personalities are completely unsurpassed!

M.H.

General Instructions

Read right through these before starting work on any of the puppets and make sure you understand them by turning to the pages and diagrams mentioned as you read.

Some notes on the knitted puppets

Knitted finger puppets are quick and very simple to make being merely one small, straight piece. Ideal even, for someone learning to knit and completely inexperienced. They take only a matter of minutes and just a few yards of wool, so what better way to use up those odds and ends? For example, the miniatures on page 30 take 4 yards (less than 4 metres) for each main part and 2 yards (less than 2 metres) for each head.

Three sizes are given, large for general family use, medium for small children's fingers and miniatures for *very* small people. However, the nature and stretch properties of knitting ensure that all three sizes will fit most people and what completely covers a toddler's finger will work well on an adult's little finger or even the tips of her other three fingers and thumb (page 31). If you like a particular character but want to make it in another size you will find this very simple to do.

All the puppets are knitted on size 12 needles.
Stocking-stitch—one row knit one row purl alternately.
Garter stitch—all plain knitting.

BASIC METHODS (Suggested colours are given on each appropriate page.)

Large size (e.g. Three Kings, page 44).
Cast on 15 sts. in double knitting wool or similar. Work 1 row in K 1, P 1 rib to prevent base curling.
Work 14 rows in stocking stitch for body.
Work 10 rows in stocking stitch for head. Do not cast off.

Medium size (e.g. Sailor, page 64).
Cast on 14 sts in 4-ply wool.
Work 24 rows in garter stitch for body.
Work 8 rows in stocking stitch for head. Do not cast off.

Miniatures (e.g. toys on page 30).
Cast on 12 sts in 3- or 4-ply wool.
Work 20 rows in garter stitch for body.
Work 7 rows in stocking stitch for head. Do not cast off.

Finishing off (all sizes).
1 Thread end of wool into a long needle and pass this through the stitches, slipping them off the

knitting needle at the same time. Pull up tightly and secure with a few stitches (top of head) (Fig 1 A).

4 Run a gathering thread round neck, pull up tightly and fasten off securely by stitching backwards and forwards through the 'neck' (B).

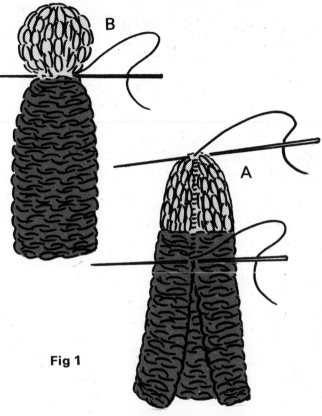

Fig 1

2 Sew up seams (centre back) (A). Turn right side out.

3 Stuff head part very firmly with a little 'knob' of cotton wool or kapok, shaping and rounding it well.

Some notes on the cards

Various ideas for using finger puppets on greetings, 'Get well soon' and baby announcement cards are given. This is an ideal way of sending an original and very inexpensive small present which is just a little more than a card and which will give hours of pleasure. The base for all the pictures is strong cardboard (a box lid?). Most are covered with material, all details of colours and textures being given in the appropriate places. Cut the material a little larger than the card and fold it round to the back, sticking it there with Copydex or similar. (This is the ideal adhesive for most sticking jobs throughout the book. Where it is not strong enough an alternative is suggested.) The easiest way to achieve flat, neat corners is as shown in Fig 2, sticking each fold as you make it.

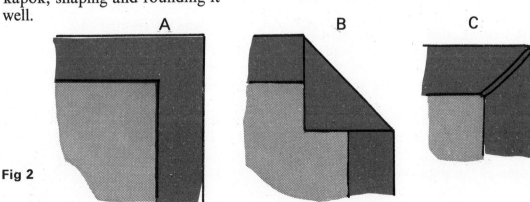

Fig 2

Many suggestions are given for making fancy edges by backing the cards with lace and braids—look through the book for ideas. These are usually stuck to the back of the picture so that only a very narrow edging shows on the front (Fig 3).

BACK

FRONT

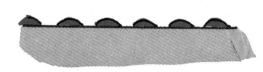

Fig 3 Sticking braid to the back of a picture.

Most of the parts which make up the pictures may be traced direct from the book and any odd pieces hidden by overlapping are easily guessed (e.g. Christmas tree, page 46).

When the picture is complete it is mounted on a piece of gay coloured card with a fold down the back (so that it opens like a book) and a letter or message can be written inside. Cut this exactly the same size as your picture but double, and stick your picture neatly and firmly in place. Bows of ribbon or cord may be tied round the fold if you wish (e.g. pages 46 and 48).

Some of the puppets slip into pockets formed by the pictures (e.g. Mary on page 48 and the little girls on page 52). When attaching the parts which form pockets, push the centre part away from the card slightly whilst sticking, so that there is plenty of room for the puppets to slip into them. The others may be fastened to the pictures by Velcro—a tiny piece of one side being stuck to the card in the appropriate place and a piece of the opposite side stuck or stitched to the back of the puppet's head. Make sure the Velcro is securely attached by using a strong adhesive such as Bostik—it can be stubborn and difficult to stick. Alternatively, the puppets can be hooked in place, the hook being stitched to the back of the head and the eye to the card. (It is of course easier to do this before sticking material to card, but not essential as the needle can be slipped along between card and felt (e.g. Christmas tree, page 46).

All the cards will fit into slim boxes in which many brands of tights arrive in the shops and which are usually readily obtainable. They can then be posted very easily.

Some notes on making hair

In most cases the puppet's hair is merely a small bundle of wool or embroidery cotton stitched to top of head. The stitches are the parting, Fig 4 A, and the hair is then arranged in the way described for each individual character. A glance through the book will give you many ideas to copy or adapt. If a fringe is needed, add a few extra strands of wool and pull some of them round to the front, stick to forehead then trim (Fig 4 B and C).

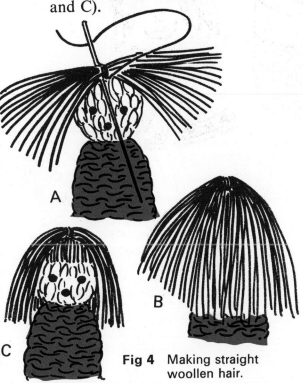

Fig 4 Making straight woollen hair.

All-over curls (Fig 5) are made by covering the head with loose looped stitches (e.g. Choirboy, pages 23 and 27). Always embroider the features first, so that the knots and

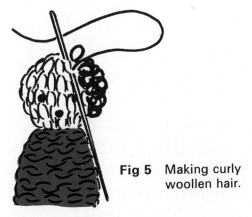

Fig 5 Making curly woollen hair.

fastening off are hidden under the hair. Bobble trimming (Fig 6) is used for some characters and is very effective and easy, details are given in the appropriate places (e.g. Clown page 75, mother page 26). If your bobbles are too large they can easily be trimmed down with small scissors. Don't discard the braid part after cutting off the bobbles—it makes a good scarf.

Fig 6 Bobble trimming.

Looped lampshade fringe (Fig 7) makes ideal long hair (e.g. brides-maid, pages 22 and 25). A small piece is merely sewn to the top of the head, the braid part at the top giving a close, curly effect and the loops forming the hair hanging down all round.

Fig 7 Looped lampshade fringe.

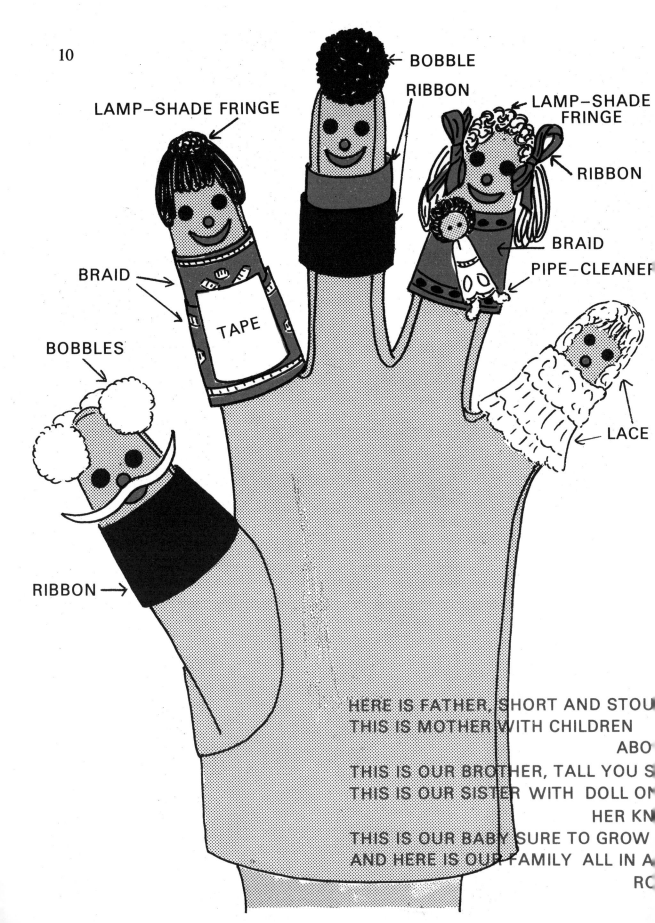

LAMP-SHADE FRINGE

BOBBLE

RIBBON

LAMP-SHADE FRINGE

RIBBON

BRAID

BRAID

PIPE-CLEANER

TAPE

BOBBLES

RIBBON →

LACE

HERE IS FATHER, SHORT AND STOU

THIS IS MOTHER WITH CHILDREN

ABO

THIS IS OUR BROTHER, TALL YOU S

THIS IS OUR SISTER WITH DOLL ON

HER KN

THIS IS OUR BABY SURE TO GROW

AND HERE IS OUR FAMILY ALL IN A

RO

The Glove Family

I expect you have often played with your fingers, pointing to each one as you said the rhyme on the opposite page—it is much more fun if you take an old glove and stick 'hair', faces and clothes to it, making each finger a member of your family. If there are a lot of you, use a pair of gloves and add grannies and aunts or a few friends and neighbours to make up the numbers. They are quick to make as there is no stitching involved. Stick the features on first, red mouths and noses and various colour eyes, with a white moustache for father. Use bobbles from bobble fringe (father has a bald patch!) and looped lampshade fringe for hair, except for the baby, which is unravelled yellow cord (or wool) stuck to the top of the little finger of the glove and covered by a lace bonnet—she also wears a lace dress. The clothes on the other members of the family are all made from ribbons, tapes or braids, with the joins down centre back. The easiest way to work is to prepare the materials then put the glove on your left hand (if it's a right-hand glove put it on back to front) and use the right hand to stick them in place. Alternatively, you could stuff the glove with paper while you work.

'Sister's' doll is merely a piece of

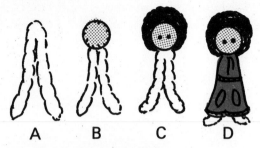

Fig 8 Making sister's doll.

pipe cleaner. Bend it in half (Fig 8 A). Nip the two 'legs' together a little and stick a small circle of pink felt to the top for a face (B). Stick a black (or yellow) bobble to back of face for hair and if it seems too big, trim it smaller. Mark two eyes with ball-point pen (C). Stick a piece of lace (or ribbon) round cleaner for a dress, leaving the ends of the cleaners showing for feet.

You can cut the fingers of the glove off and use them separately if you like or leave them joined and wear the glove as it is.

There are lots of other people you could make from an old glove—your teacher and some of the children in your class perhaps, or a wedding group. You will find many ideas to help you in other sections of this book.

THUMBOLD	THUMB HE	TOM THUMBKIN
THIBITY–THOLD	WIZBEE	WILLIE WILKIN
LANGMAN	LONG MAN	LONG DANIEL
LICK PAN	CHERRY TREE	BETTY BODKIN
WEE MAN	LITTLE JACK DANDY	LITTLE DICK

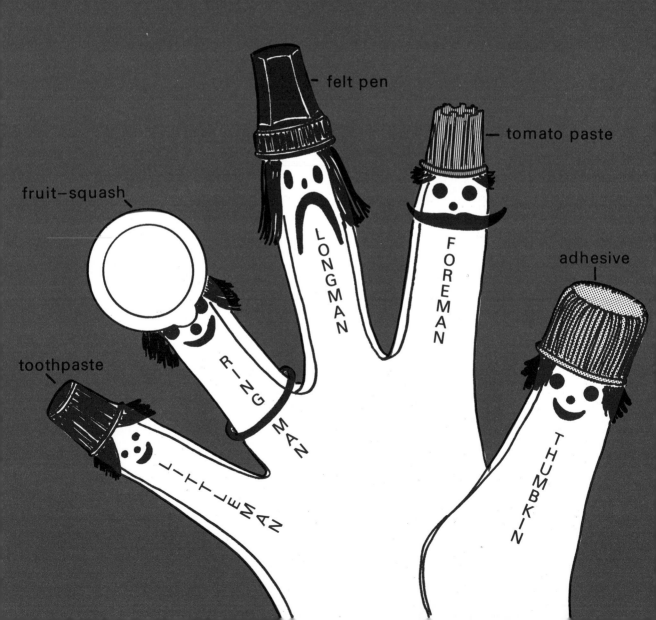

felt pen

tomato paste

fruit–squash

adhesive

toothpaste

LONGMAN

FOREMAN

RING MAN

THUMBKIN

LITTLE MAN

Five Merry Little Men

I wonder if you know the names which have been given to our fingers over the years? There are three traditional lists on the opposite page and it is easy to see how many of them grew up—'lick pan', what a lovely name! Mothers used to play with their babies' fingers, wiggling each one in turn as they gave it a name.

Do you know this rhyme?

Thumbkin says I'll dance,
Thumbkin says I'll sing,
Dance and sing you merry little men,
Thumbkin says I'll dance and sing.

Foreman says I'll dance, .
Foreman says I'll sing,
Dance and sing you merry little men,
Foreman says I'll dance and sing.

Longman says I'll dance,
Longman says I'll sing,
Dance and sing you merry little men,
Longman says I'll dance and sing.

Ringman says I'll dance,
Ringman says I'll sing,
Dance and sing you merry little men,
Ringman says I'll dance and sing.

Littleman says I'll dance,
Littleman says I'll sing,
Dance and sing you merry little men,
Littleman says I'll dance and sing.

You wiggle each finger in turn and make it dance as you sing or say it's own particular verse.

It's fun on a wet day to take an old glove and turn each finger into a little man. I used bundles of wool stuck to the top of the fingers for hair and caps from bottles and tubes stuck on top of the hair for hats. The features were felt.

Try to bring out the character of each finger—giving 'Littleman' small eyes and mouth and a little hat, 'Longman' a long hat and a long droopy moustache and making 'Foreman' look important. You will easily think of lots of ideas of your own.

Our Fat Black Cat

This is a game to play with very small brothers and sisters.

1 Find an old pair of black gloves, some scraps of black, white, green and pink felt and some stiff white thread.

2 Cut out felt features as shown in the picture.

3 Slip one glove on to your hand, clench your fist and tuck in your thumb to make mother cat's head. Mark positions with pins or chalk then remove glove and stick on ears, pink nose, white eyes, green iris and black pupils. Embroider white mouth and whiskers.

4 Lay the other glove flat on a table, palm upwards and stick features to all five fingers for the kittens. Embroider mouths. Pull threads through for whiskers,

secure with a spot of gum or colourless nail varnish to stop them pulling out.

These gloves will be of a large size because they are black but that doesn't matter at all for acting out the rhyme.

If you have an old pair of gloves that fit your hand well—any colour —make both gloves up into kitten puppets and try playing cat's cradle with them whilst wearing them— it's quite difficult!

OUR FAT BLACK CAT –one fist
HAS FIVE NEW KITTENS–hold up fingers, other hand.
BECAUSE SHE LOVES THEM
THEY FIT ROUND HER LIKE MITTENS.–fit fingers over fist
SSH! SSH! SSH!
THEY ARE ALL ASLEEP ,
WE'LL HAVE ONE QUICK LOOK
THEN AWAY WE'LL CREEP.

Two Grand People

Two grand people met in a lane, (1)
Bowed most politely and
bowed once again, (2)
How do you do and
how do you do, (3)
And how do you do again. (4)

FEATHERS

BUTTONS

FRINGE

RIBBON

FINGER
OF A
GLOVE

RIBBON

BOBBLES

SEQUINS

FUR

FINGER OF A
GLOVE

Have you ever played this game
with your fingers? You hold up
your two index fingers quite a long
way apart then bring them
together (1). Bend the fingers
slowly towards each other twice (2).
Bend first one and then the other (3)
then bend them slowly towards
each other again (4).

If you have some very worn gloves
with two good fingers, cut these off
and taking your ideas from this
picture, make 'two grand people',
to use as puppets. Mine were very
grand indeed and I used all sorts
of things to dress them up.

Three baby announcement cards (and three babies!).
The tea party.
Some Indians.
A Hula-Hooping clown.
Two dressed felt puppets.

Four and twenty blackbirds baked in a pie for a party tea table centre piece.

Finger puppets for Christmas.
A selection of Christmas cards.
Dressed felt puppets.
Eskimos.
The three Kings.

A sweater for the very
young with puppets in the
pockets. In the large paper
boat some dressed felt puppets.

A Never-never Duck

1 Take an old glove, white or yellow if possible.

2 Cut a small circle of soft, matching material (stockinette from an old sock or Tee shirt is ideal). Gather all round the edge, taking a small turning at the same time. Pull up the gathers a little and stuff to form a knob (the head).

3 Put the glove on your left hand. (If you are an adult making the duck for a child, slip your little finger into the thumb of the small glove.) Push thumb of glove (neck) into the base of head, pull up gathers to fit and stitch head to thumb of glove, working all round the base several times.

4 Stitch a small black bead or button to each side for eyes, working right through from side to side and pulling stitches tightly.

5 Cut a yellow felt beak and smearing a little Copydex along edge, stick or stitch it to head.

6 Stick one or two small feathers to back of head for a crest. (Add some to the fingers, too, if you want a feathery tail.)

7 Hide your hand behind a table or chair and wiggle it about—you will get some fantastic effects.

Make another duck for the other hand but vary his expression by giving him different-shaped eyes and beak.

Ten Little Indians

Ten little Indians standing in a line,
One toddled home and then there
were nine;
Nine little Indians swinging on a
gate,
One tumbled off and then there
were eight.

Eight little Indians gayest under
heaven,
One went to sleep and then there
were seven;
Seven little Indians cutting up their
tricks,
One broke his neck and then there
were six.

Six little Indians kicking all alive,
One kicked the bucket and then
there were five;
Five little Indians on a cellar door,
One tumbled in and then there were
four.

Four little Indians up on a spree,
One he got fuddled and then there
were three;
Three little Indians out in a canoe,
One tumbled overboard and then
there were two.

Two little Indians fooling with a
gun,
One shot the other and then there
was one;
One little Indian living all alone,
He got married and then there were
none.

Do you know this version of the
famous counting rhyme? It is very
old and although it was written by
an Englishman, I am told it is still
remembered by American children.

These Red Indian finger puppets
(some are shown in colour plate
opposite page 16) appear to be
wrapped in blankets, are quick to
make and form the basis for a
game. Ten people in a class could
each make one puppet or a Brownie
or Cub pack could co-operate.

You will need

Scraps of tailor's canvas or similar stiff, non-fraying material in a neutral colour for body.
Buckram or card for the feathers.
Scraps of brown felt for hands.
Black wool for hair and bright colours for head bands.
Black, brown and gay coloured felt pens for colouring.
Ten pipe cleaners for making finger grips.

How to make each puppet

1 Cut out the main piece in canvas, tracing it from Fig 9.

2 Body Using felt pens mark the front fold of blanket, eyes and nose in black, colour the face brown, leaving a space round edge of eyes so that they show up well and draw a bright border round the lower edge (Fig 9). Take a few stitches in red embroidery cotton for war paint, if you wish (see page 18).

Fig 9 Basic body shape.

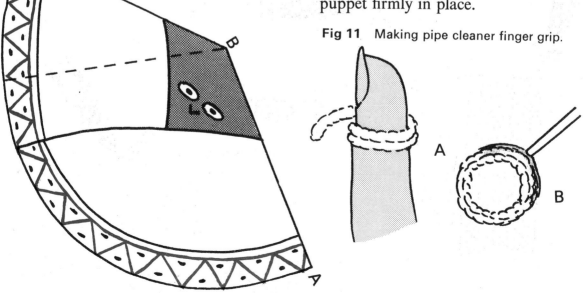

3 Spread adhesive over the triangle C–B–A and roll the piece into a cone so that the A's match. Press firmly in place.

4 Fold the top point over to the back and stick in place (Fig 10).

BACK

Fig 10 Folding top of head.

5 Finger grip (Fig 11) Roll a pipe cleaner round and round your little finger (if an adult making for a child) or round a finger roughly the size of intended user, tucking and pinching the ends in (A). Spread adhesive round the outside edge of the ring thus made (B). Slip the pipe cleaner ring on to your forefinger and gently insert this finger into the puppet (C) pushing it upwards until it fits the cone. Pull your finger out, leaving the pipe cleaner ring inside (D). When dry, this ring will grip almost any size of finger and hold the puppet firmly in place.

Fig 11 Making pipe cleaner finger grip.

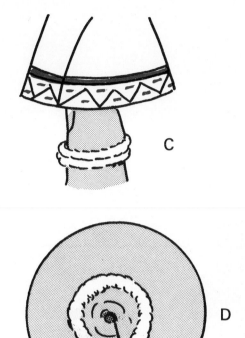

C

D

6 *Hair* Spread a little adhesive over top of head and lay six strands of black wool across from side to side. When dry, plait and stick to front of puppet to secure ends. Trim off surplus wool.

7 *Feathers* Cut these from buckram or something stiff, mark with gay coloured felt pens and stick to back of head. Bind head with a piece of bright coloured wool for head-band, tying or stitching ends at back.

8 *Hand* Cut this from brown felt and stick in place. Make nine more puppets in the same way, then give each a tiny symbol corresponding

with this or your own favourite version of the rhyme.

Page 19 shows you how I identified my Indians. The gate is made from pieces of matchstick and the bucket is the cap off a toothpaste tube with a piece of wool stuck in place for a handle. I cut the canoe, door and gun from thin card and painted them and stuck a little ring to the hand of the one who got married. I had to indicate the Indian who went to sleep and the one who got 'fuddled' by giving them different shaped eyes and I just couldn't think how to show that one had broken his neck except by bending him sideways and sticking him in that position! I left the Indian who toddled home quite plain.

A game for two very small people to play with these Indians
1 Put the puppets in a pile behind your back or shut your eyes.
2 Each take an Indian in turn and put them on your left hand (five each).
3 Say the rhyme together and as you mention each Indian the person who happens to have that particular one on his hand must take him off.
4 The winner is the person who has the last Indian on his finger.

You could make a large canvas cone for a wigwam for your Indians, or a totem pole from cotton reels and paint both these in bright colours. Keep them all on a green, felt-covered board whilst not in use.

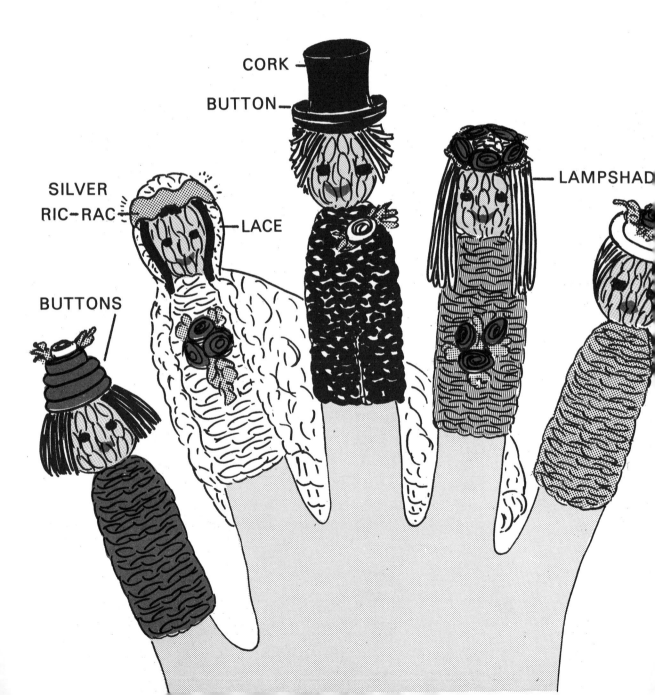

CORK

BUTTON

SILVER
RIC-RAC

LACE

LAMPSHAD

BUTTONS

A Wedding Group

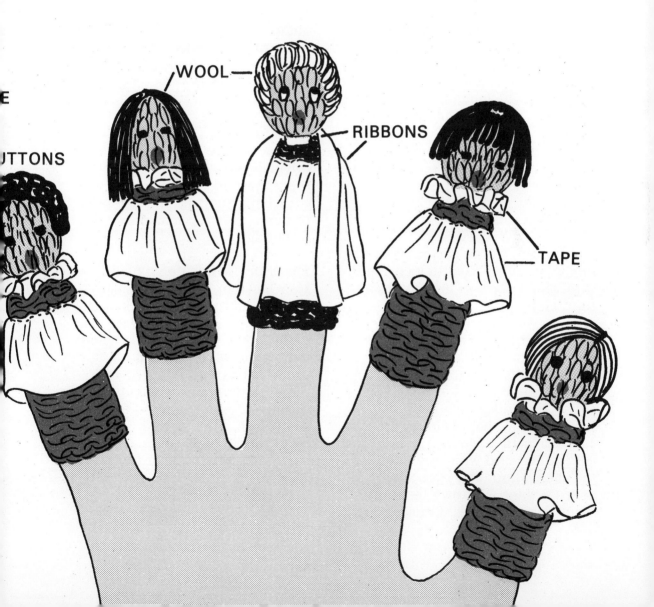

WOOL

RIBBONS

TAPE

...UTTONS

A wedding with a fairy princess bride is magic to all generations and its chief participants make an enchanting set of finger puppets which adapt themselves ideally for turning into an extended present for a sick child, or for an older child to make for herself whilst ill. Only the basic characters are given here but the idea can be stretched or shrunk at will. Having made the bridegroom, it is a simple matter to add the best man, bride's father and male guests varying them by giving some grey morning suits and toppers instead of black. The number of choir-boys and brides-maids can be altered and some of them made very small by using the pattern for the miniature puppets on page 6. Having made the two mothers, innumerable female guests can be added by changing the colour of their dresses and shape of their hats—the button box is a wonderful source of supply for glamorous hats!

The puppets can be presented in two ways, either fixed to a covered card with Velcro, as though posing for a group photograph (in the same way as the snow scene on page 50) or placed as though standing in church at the actual ceremony (see colour plate opposite page 33) (although of course the bridegroom doesn't *really* wear his hat in church!). For this method, cover a strip of very strong card with grey felt for the church floor and stick a strip of red or blue felt down the centre for the carpeted aisle. Collect a lot

of slim cotton spools (Drima or Gütermann) and firmly glue one to the place where you want each character to stand. The puppets will fit securely over the spools and can be kept standing on the board when not in play (a most useful talking point for visiting doctors, therapists and nurses). Start by sending the board containing one puppet, then follow up by posting a new character each day—one for each day of the small patient's stay in hospital. If possible, try to arrange for the bride, groom, guests, etc, to arrive in the correct order of appearance, the vicar and choir-boys first, bride and bridesmaids last.

All the wedding puppets are made to the medium-sized patterns on page 6, but the body parts of the originals were knitted in double knitting wool. All the flowers were cut from a short length of rose-bud trimming—or they could be cut from felt.

The bride White dress, pink head. Hair black or brown lampshade fringe. Embroider blue eyes, red mouth. Veil—wide white lace or a scrap of net. Stitch this to top of head, to sides of face and all round back of neck. Catch each side to bottom of dress and leave surplus length hanging to form a short train. Make the coronet from silver ric-rac braid (or any silver trimming). Sew three or four rosebuds and leaves to centre of dress for bouquet.

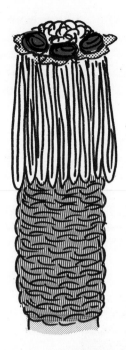

The bridesmaids   Make exactly as bride but use any pretty colour for dresses and a different colour fringe for hair (yellow?). Omit the veil and add a circlet of rosebud trimming round head.

The bridegroom Black body (morning suit). Pink face. Blue or black eyes. Red mouth. Brown wool hair (a short bundle sewn to top of head, smoothed round and stuck in place). Hat, stitch an upward-curving black button to top of head for brim. Cover a small cork with black felt for crown and stick securely to button. Take a long white stitch at centre of lower part of body to give the appearance of dividing for trousers. Stitch one flower in place for buttonhole.

The mothers Dresses any bright colour, pink faces, blue, brown or black eyes, red mouth. Make hair in two different colours and styles. Originals had one short, brown hairstyle made like the bridegroom's and one black which was a small bundle sewn to top of head and caught at the back in nape of neck. Her large 'bun' was a black bobble cut from bobble fringing, sewn high up to back of head. Hats are piles of buttons sewn to tops of heads, topped by a small flower.

The Vicar Black body for cassock, rosy pink rather florid face. Blue, brown or black eyes with whites showing at base (eyes raised to heaven!), round, red, 'singing' mouth. White hair is a series of stitches taken round head in a ring, leaving a bald pate at the back. Surplice is wide, white ribbon; stole, very narrow white ribbon or tape. Dog collar showing at front from inside cassock is a tiny patch of white tape sewn in place.

the one inevitably very long-haired character. Surplice, gathered wide white tape or ribbon. Ruff—very narrow white tape or ribbon gathered to make a frill round neck.

N.B. For children in hospital, always *post* as opposed to taking presents so as to break up the day— these puppets will fit in an envelope.

The choirboys Red, purple or black bodies for cassocks. Faces in varying coloured pinks, some pale, some bright—red mouths, various coloured eyes. Hair all different colours, brown, black, yellow (and don't forget ginger) and in different styles. Tiny looped curls, straight stitches to give a newly plastered-down effect, short block cuts and

The Hospital Ward

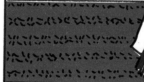

(A 'Get well soon' card which is also an extended present holding three or four puppets—see colour plate opposite page 33.)

The idea of this card is to send it in good time so that it is waiting for the patient when he or she arrives in hospital—maybe to have tonsils out.

1 Choose a piece of light-coloured card suitable for the wall—this forms the base. Stick a piece of check paper in place for floor tiles. Stick an edging of ric-rac to back. Stick a rectangle of white card in place for locker. Cut a vase from coloured felt or card and stick in place. Cut a few flowers from a magazine and stick above vase.

2 Cut the pillow from a piece of card, making it long enough to go well down into the bed. Cover with a piece of white cotton material, sticking at back. Stick pillow in place. Cut white plastic drinking straws to size and stick securely in place for bed head.

3 Cut a piece of candlewick for bed-cover, making it about ½ inch longer and 1 inch (2·5 cm.) wider than picture. Turn these extra pieces back at base and sides and stick. Cover top edge with a piece of white material for sheet sticking it at back and sides. Stick completed bedclothes to card, leaving a free portion in centre to make a pocket for the puppet. Cut more drinking straws and stick in place for end of bed. Make a little book from a piece of folded card with a picture on the front. Stick the back to bed, leaving the front loose and open.

4 Knit all the puppets as given for the medium size on page 6.
Little girl (You can see her out of bed on page 36.) A pretty coloured 'body' for nightie, pink face, blue eyes, red mouth, and hair to match that of whoever you are making the card for. Sew a little bundle of wool to top of head, smooth it round, stick band neatly in place, then stick hair and trim.

5 *Matron* Navy blue dress, black tape belt, white tape collar. (Make a buckle from a tiny piece of filigree silver-coloured metal cut from an old brooch.) Embroider red mouth, black eyes. Sew a bundle of long grey wool to top of head for hair. Spread a little adhesive to head, smooth hair backwards. Plait, twist into a bun and stitch, tucking the end well in. (See back of nurse on opposite page.) Cut a rectangle of white cotton material 2½ inches (6·5 cm.) long and 2 inches (5 cm.) wide for cap. Fold back one long edge twice for front and crease well to keep in place. Smear a little adhesive round top of head and press cap in place round front edge. Fold cap at back and stick firmly in place.

6 *Nurses* Make as Matron, giving them whatever colour dress you wish, aprons cut from white cotton material and a sequin for a watch.

7 Fasten the nurses to the card with scraps of Velcro.

8 Cut the mount a little larger than your picture and choose a pretty coloured piece of card for this so that it forms a frame when you stick your picture in place.

A Chest of Drawers Full of Puppet Dolls

This is an ideal extended present for a child in hospital—have the chest containing one doll awaiting the young patient's arrival, then post another doll each day. The original chest had ten drawers so that there was one puppet for each finger—it is a good idea to try to make a drawer for each day the small patient is expected to be away from home (see colour plate opposite page 32).

To make the chest

Simply stick the matchboxes together as required, either in twos or in a single tall column. In this case it is a good idea to make a little base of thick card to help balance it, then cover the outside of the front of each drawer with gay Fablon or Contact, or similar. Stick a strip of Sellotape or Scotch

TRANSPAREN
TAPE

tape completely round the outside edge of each drawer (after putting on Contact and before sewing on handle (No 2 below) for added strength and to help them slide in and out. Stitch on bead or button handles using strong thread and tying the ends off inside. Cover the knot with a small piece of adhesive tape. Be sure to make a good strong job of the chest as there's nothing more frustrating for a sick child than being given a fragile toy which breaks with handling and having no one around to mend it.

The dolls

Knit all these as given on page 6 for miniatures.

1 Soldier Lower half of body black, upper half red. Head, four rows pink, remainder black. Embroider black eyes, red mouth, white buttons.

2 Clown Gay striped body, white face. White ribbon ruff. Embroider black eyes, red mouth and nose. Make hair from three black bobbles from bobble fringe as given for Punch's clown on page 75.

3 Schoolgirl doll Lower half of body navy blue, upper half white, pink face, blue eyes, red mouth. Sew a little bundle of wool to top of head for hair, smooth downward and catch each side, stitching to

32

side of face. Plait ends tightly and bind or stitch to secure. Tie on a piece of narrow tape or ribbon for bows and stitch a piece to front of blouse for a tie.

4 Red Riding Hood doll Exactly as baby doll (No 8) but use red wool. Add a few yellow loops at front of face for hair.

5 Little girl doll Bright body. Pink face. Blue eyes, red mouth. Sew a little bundle of wool to top of head for hair. Smooth backwards to nape of head, stitching in place. Tie with a small bow at back. Trim.

6 Toddler doll Red body. Work 5 rows in st st for face then break off pink wool and join in red again. P 5 rows. K 1 row. P 1 row. (This makes a woolly hat.) Finish off as usual. Make blue eyes and red mouth. Work tiny loops of yellow wool over sides and back of pink part for hair. Tie a narrow piece of braid or similar round neck for a scarf and stitch.

7 Mother doll Work exactly as for little girl but use different colours and make hair longer.

Plait this at back, twist on to top of head to make a 'bun', tuck end in and stitch securely in place.

8 Baby doll White body, pink face. Embroider blue eyes, red mouth. To make the bonnet, cast on 12 stitches. K 12 rows. Do not cast off. Break off wool and thread end into a darning needle, slip the needle and wool through the stitches, pulling them off knitting needle at the same time. Pull up tightly and fasten off (centre back). Tie a narrow piece of ribbon round the baby's neck, having a tiny bow under chin. Slip bonnet on to head and stitch firmly in place as necessary.

Some of the birds perched on a tree for a party tea table centre piece. Thimble-
Thumbelina in front.
A chest of drawers full of miniature puppets.
On the hand: Tom Thimble-Thumb, the cow with the crumpled horn, and a
leaping hare. In front a hopping frog.

Some puppets for use in hospital. The wedding group.
A 'Get well soon' card. Two 'cover-ups' for bandaged fingers.

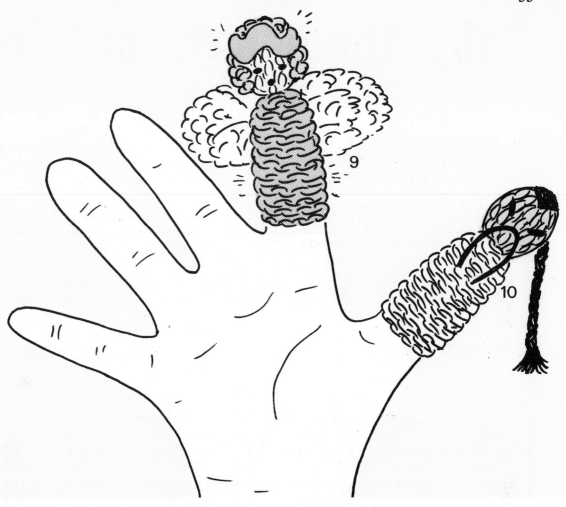

9 Fairy doll Silver yarn body (Goldfinger or similar), pink face. Yellow looped hair. Silver ric-rac coronet. White lace wings. Embroider blue eyes, red mouth.

10 Chinaman doll Bright coloured body. Yellow face. Embroider black eyes. Sew piece of black wool in place for moustache. Sew a little bundle of black wool to top of head hanging down back. Plait this for about 2 inches (5 cm.). Secure ends with a few stitches and trim.

The dolls curl up quite easily in matchbox drawers.

Baby Announcement Cards

The card pictured below and those on pages 35 and 36 are designed for a mother to send home from hospital as a gift to the small boy or girl left at home and to announce the arrival of a new brother or sister. Alternatively, children might like to make some of these to send to favourite cousins or special friends when a new baby arrives. Scraps of wool and lace over from the baby's layette can be used up in this way. (See colour plate opposite page 16.)

The baby in the bath

Cover the card with pretty flowered material and edge with braid (see general instructions). Trace the bath and cut out in white felt marking rim with ball point pen. Cut a slit where the baby sits and stick bath to the card by the edge only, thus forming a pocket for the puppet. Knit the puppet all in pale pink wool as given for miniatures on page 6. Embroider a few strands of yellow hair, blue eyes and red mouth, then sit him in the bath.

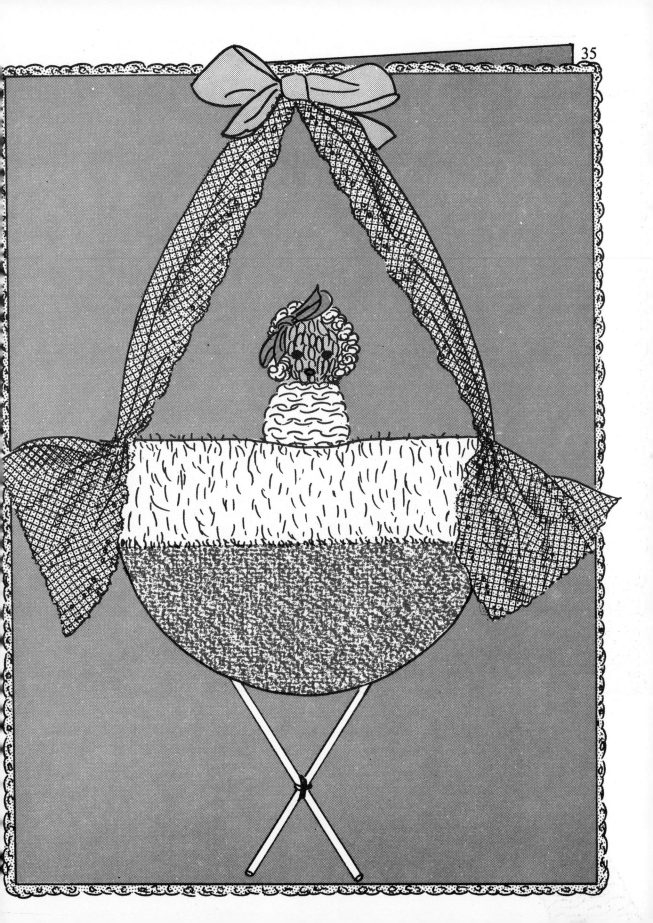

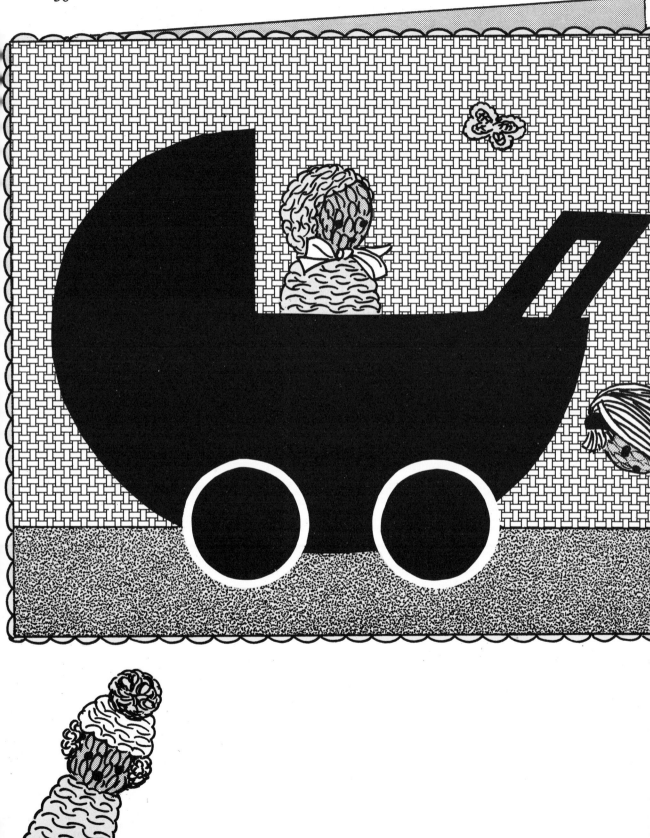

The little girl in the cot

Cover the card with a pretty, plain coloured material and edge with lace (see general instructions). Stick two cocktail sticks in place for legs of cot and stitch where they cross. Trace cot and cut out in old pink blanket or similar. Stick a strip of white fur fabric trimming (or plain material for a sheet) across top, turning raw edge to back and sticking. Stick cot to card by edges only, thus forming a pocket for the puppet. Stick lace in place for drapes, arranging it carefully and gathering in at top and sides by stitching. Tie a bow of ribbon and stick to top. Knit the puppet as given for the baby on page 32, but omit the bonnet and cover her head with looped stitches of stranded cotton for hair. Make a little bow and stick to head. Embroider blue eyes and red mouth.

The baby in the pram

Choose a piece of plain coloured material for background but do not cover card yet. Trace and cut out pram in black felt. Stick to background material except for top edge and sufficient depth to make a pocket for the baby. Sew two large, shanked black buttons in place for wheels. Cover card and back it with ric-rac (see general instructions). Cut a strip of sandpaper for path, cutting to shape of base of pram and stick in place slipping under wheels. Cut a butterfly from a piece of daisy trimming and stick in place. Knit the puppet as given for the baby on page 32 and sit her in the pram.

In case you prefer a baby boy an idea is given below the card (or you might need one of each for twins). Knit this puppet in the same way as the girl but omit the bonnet and knit the top half of the head in yellow or white wool, working in garter stitch to make a hat. Sew a bobble to the top and give him a few curls of looped stitches.

You might like to make yourself (or Mummy might like to make you), as well as the baby. The little girl shown here is like the one in bed on page 28, but shows you her side view and knitted in garter stitch. She could be fixed to any of the cards, standing beside the cot, pram or bath by sticking a tiny piece of Velcro, one side to the back of her head and the other to the card so that she could be pressed in place and pulled off again.

Two 'Cover-Ups' for Bandaged Fingers

Frightfully Fat Freddie.   Fearfully Fat Freda.

Frightfully Fat Freddie and
Fearfully Fat Freda fit snugly over
a bandaged or splintered finger,
keeping the dressing clean and
comfortable. (See colour plate
opposite page 33.)

How to make them

1 Knit and make up both as
given for the large puppets on
page 6 using bright colours for the
clothes and pink for the heads, but
cast on 20 stitches and work the
bodies in garter stitch as this is
more elastic. Make the bodies
whatever length you need.

2 Arms Cast on 4 stitches.
K 12 rows. Break off coloured
wool and join in pink. Work 4
rows in stocking stitch.
Next row: p 2 tog twice.
Next row: k 2.
Next row: k 2 tog.
Sew the arms firmly in place in
whatever position you prefer—first
at shoulders then all round hands.

3 Freddie's polo collar Cast on
8 stitches. K 24 rows. Cast off.
Sew to Freddie all round neck,
turned upwards to cover face. Join
centre back seam and roll down so
that collar is double.

4 Hair Look through the book
and use whichever style you prefer
providing it is neat and trim. (A
cover-up puppet must not have any
loose, untidy bits and pieces to get
in the way.) In the picture,
Freddie's was a small bundle of
wool sewn to the top of his head,
then smoothed round, stuck in
place and trimmed. Freda's was
very long. It was sewn to the top of
her head, smoothed down at each
side and stuck, then gathered into
the nape of her neck and stitched.
The ends were made into one plait,
brought up the back of her head
and firmly twisted and stitched into
a bun on the top.

An 'Exerciser' for Post-bandage Therapy

An injured finger needs exercising once the splint or bandage is removed. A leaping hare to slip on the finger is a help and soon overcomes the stiffness.

EAR

How to make him

1 Using brown wool and garter stitch throughout knit and make up a medium size puppet as given on page 6.

2 Trace, cut out and stick on white felt eyes and black pupils, embroider black nose.

3 Using black button thread make whiskers as given for the mice on page 80.

4 Stick a white bobble to back for tail.

5 Trace and cut out two pink and two brown felt ears. Stick together in pairs (pink is lining). Fold base inwards and stick. Sew firmly to top of head.

Round about there,
Sat a little hare,
The dogs came and chased him
Right up there!

I expect you know that old rhyme —you can play the finger game wearing the hare, next time you are having fun with a baby.

The colour plate opposite page 32 shows this hare as well as a bright green hopping frog, which also makes a good exerciser. He is a medium sized puppet worked in stocking stitch and has felt limbs and bead eyes.

Toe 'Plaster Puppets'—
A School of Owls

These appear on the tree in the colour plate opposite page 32.

Finger (and toe) puppets are a tremendous help in overcoming the tedium of long weeks with limbs in plaster. My own small granddaughter immediately 'made friends' with her grandfather's broken leg and its strange heavy sheath when the owls shown below appeared on his toes! Long hours of amusement followed for both patient and visitor when the puppets were sometimes on Emma's fingers and sometimes on 'Grampie's' toes. Toes of course can't be wiggled separately and the entire class had to move in unison.

How to make them

1   The baby owls   Knit in brown speckly wool as given for the miniature puppets on page 6, knitting only 20 rows for the bodies.

2   The large owl   Knit in the same wool, complete with tail and wings, as given for the blackbird on page 56.

3   Trace the features from the picture and stick to faces. Stick tiny zig-zag pieces of yellow felt to lower edges for claws.

4   Make the mortarboard for the large owl from a tiny square of cardboard covered with black felt and the tassel from a little bundle of black embroidery cotton stitched to centre of mortarboard by a long, hanging thread. Stick firmly to head with plenty of adhesive, pressing well on.

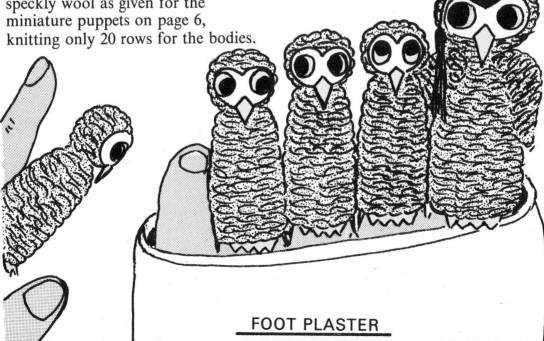

FOOT PLASTER

Finger 'Plaster Puppets'— Eskimos and a Seal

The Eskimos appear in the colour plate opposite page 17.

Small fingers emerging from a plaster encasing a broken arm often have to be wiggled and exercised— a puppet family is a great help. These Eskimos live in an igloo made from half a coconut painted white and with a door cut out of it, when not on duty—the plaster on the arm is the snow and ice!

Eskimos

Knit as given for baby on page 32 but use fawn wool for the face. Embroider black hair, eyes and lacings, red nose and mouth. Stick a scrap of white fur fabric round the edge of bonnet.

Seal

Cast on 16 stitches in fawn double knitting wool. Knit until the piece is square. Cast off. Fold the piece in half cornerwise and join edges from one corner downwards for nose end and the opposite corner upwards for tail end, leaving a gap in the centre for the thumb. Turn

the other two corners up for flippers, keeping them up with a few stitches through the lower edge, if necessary. Embroider black nose and eyes.

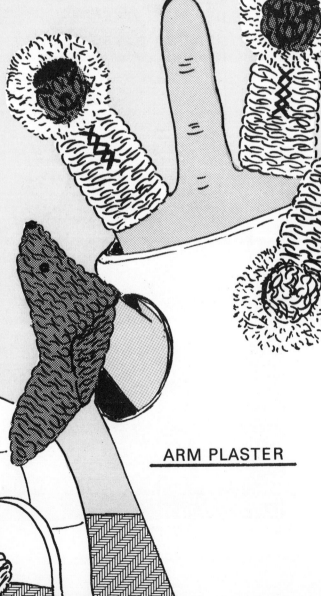

ARM PLASTER

Father Christmas Arrives

A Christmas card holding two puppets. More ideas are given on pages 44–5, 46–7, 48–9 and 54.

See colour plate opposite page 17.

1 Cover top half of card with material suitable for wallpaper, bottom half with felt. Stick a strip of white paper over join for skirting board. Edge with lace. Stick a scrap of fur fabric for rug.

2 Trace foot of bed, headboard, window sill and frame. Cut out in wood-grain Fablon or Contact. Stick rectangle of black paper for sky. Add window sill and frame and scraps of lace frilling for curtains. Cut some far-distant views from old Christmas cards and fold in half to make miniature cards. Stick in place by backs only so that the fronts are loose and they appear to be standing on window sill.

3 Cut pillow from white card and stick lace round edge at back. Stick headboard then pillow in place. Trace and cut out blanket. Tuck a piece of broderie anglaise over top for sheet, stick at back. Turn raw sides in and stick. Stick foot of bed to post-card to strengthen, then stick it to blanket. Stick blanket and foot of bed to card, leaving a free section in the centre.

4 Cut two stocking shapes from a pair of tights, oversew them together on the wrong side. Make a hem round top. Turn right side out and stick to bed head.

5 Knit the little girl as given for large size puppets on page 6, giving her a pretty nightie and pink head. Embroider red mouth, blue eyes. Sew bundle of yellow wool to top of head, smooth down and stitch to each side of head. Plait tightly so that the pigtails curl up. Stitch ends to stop them unravelling and tie on two bows.

6 Knit Father Christmas as given on page 54 and fasten him to the card with Velcro.

You will find this card looks much more attractive when made up than it does in this picture because you can use brilliant colours and jewels.

The Three Kings

See colour plate opposite page 17.

long piece at the top, stick one over the other to form dunes, then stick the completed piece to the card by the three straight edges only (for about 1 inch (2·5 cm.) inwards) thus forming a pocket.

2   Stick a silver card or foil star in place. Paint streaks of clear gum radiating from the star. Sprinkle silver glitter over them, tap card to shake off surplus.

3   Knit the kings as given for the large size puppets on page 6, giving each one a different coloured body (red, green and purple perhaps) and making one face yellow, one brown and one pink. To make the ermine edging on robes, cast on in double white wool.

1st row: join in double black wool for ermine tails. K 1 white, 1 black, (2 white, 1 black) 4 times, 1 white. Break off black wool.
2nd row: P.
3rd row: K, carry on with main colour.

4   *Oriental King*   Yellow face, a long black felt moustache, black slit eyes and a black wool pigtail.

Coloured King   Brown face, black wool loops for hair, white eyes with black pupils, red nose and mouth.

White King   Pink face, grey hair stitched in bundle to top of head, brown eyes, red nose and mouth.

5   Stick a different type of glittery braid round each head for a crown and sew a gift to the front of each robe—shiny gilt, silver or diamanté buckles or buttons are ideal.

1   Cover the board with a glowing midnight blue silk or velvet for the night sky. Edge with braid at back (see general instructions). Cut several pieces of coarse sandpaper for the desert. Starting with one

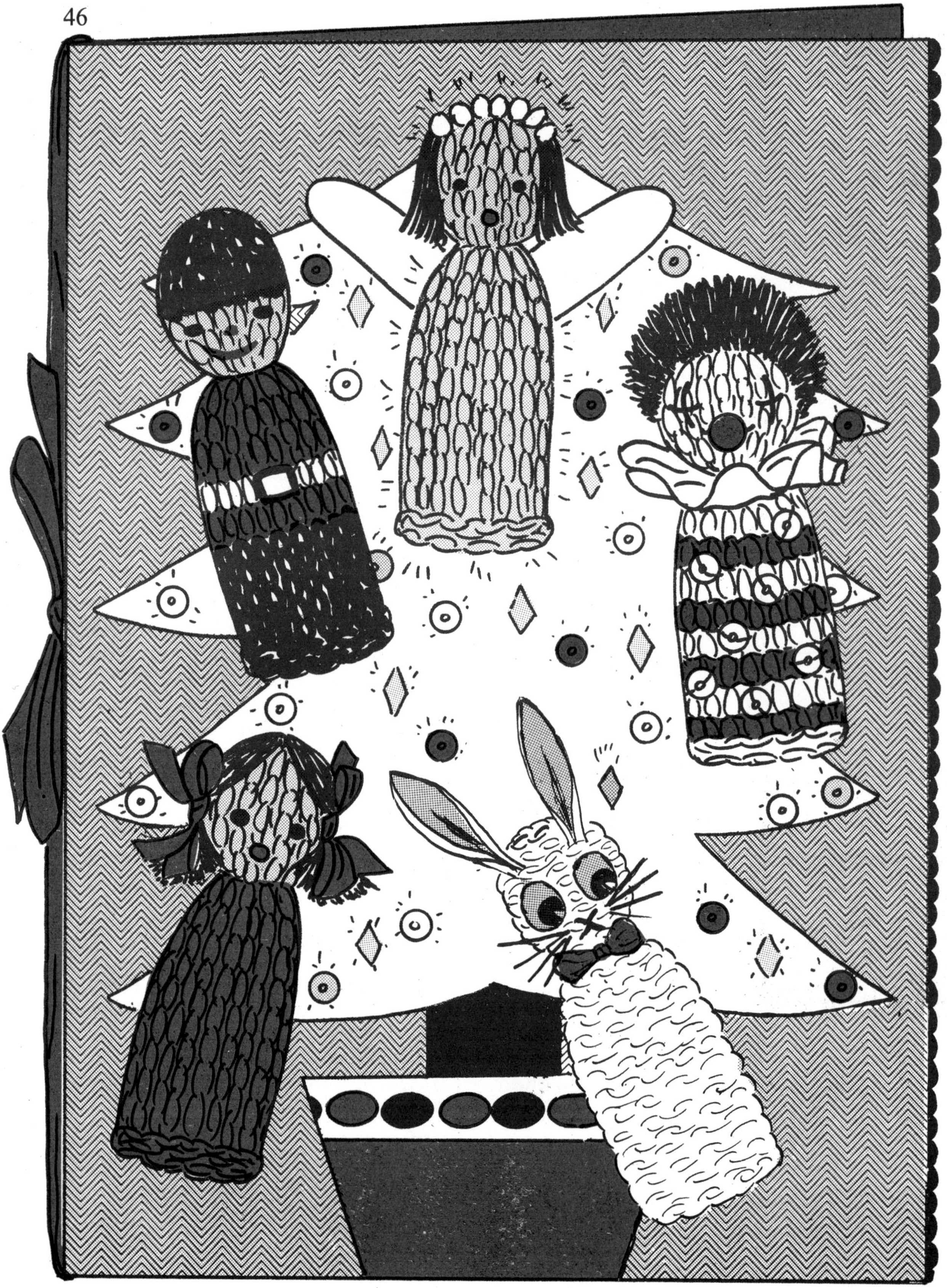

The Christmas Tree

See colour plate opposite page 17.

1 Cover card with suitable background material. Stick braid down one edge, at back (see general instructions). Trace and cut tree in vivid green felt, tree trunk in brown, tub in red. Stick a piece of decorative braid along top of tub —cutting ends to shape, stick trunk and tub to card.

2 Decide where to hang your puppets when you have made them and sew one hook part of a hook and eye to the tree for each puppet, in a place where it will eventually be hidden by their heads. Stick tree in place. Decorate it by sticking coloured sequins and diamond- or star-shaped pieces of foil or silver lamé here and there.

3 Knit all the puppets, except the toy rabbit, as given for the large size on page 6, with the following details.

4 *Clown* Striped body, white face. Embroider black crosses for eyes, sew on a large red bead for nose, stick a scrap of black fur to top of head for hair. Make frill from white ribbon or tape joined into a ring and gathered along one edge. Decorate body with sequins.

5 *Doll* Coloured body, pink face. Embroider blue eyes, red mouth. Sew a little bundle of wool to the top of head for hair, smooth downwards and stitch at each side to form bunches. Trim. Tie on two bright coloured, narrow ribbon bows.

6 *Toy rabbit* Make this exactly as given for the hare on page 39 but use white wool and pink felt for the eyes. It is better not to give him a tail because the bobble would prevent him from hanging flat against the tree. You can tie a narrow bow of ribbon round his neck if you like.

7 *Soldier* Lower half black, top half red, with a white stripe for belt. Lower half of head pink for face, top half black for busby. Embroider blue eyes, red mouth and nose, yellow buckle.

8 *Fairy* Body silver or white wool with a silver Lurex thread. Pink face. Embroider blue eyes, red mouth. Sew a bundle of yellow wool or embroidery cotton for hair then smooth round head, sticking neatly in place with Copydex. Trim. Sew a piece of diamanté trimming or silver braid or sequins to head. Trace and cut out wings in white Vilene or similar and stick in place.

9 Sew the eye part of the hooks and eyes to the backs of the puppets' heads and hang them on the hooks on the tree.

10 Mount the card in the usual way and finish off with a gay piece of ribbon round fold of card, tied in a bow at the back edge.

The Nativity

1 Cover card with plain homespun-looking material.

2 Trace and cut out window frame and manger in wood-grain Fablon or Contact. Stick a piece of black or navy blue Fablon to back of window frame for night sky.

See colour plate opposite page 17.

Stick completed piece in place. Add a silver foil star.

3 Cut halos in gold, yellow, or silver card (chocolate boxes?), wings in white card. Stick large

halo to back of manger with a few strands of wood wool (fine shavings) caught between them and strengthen with a backing of thin card. Stick manger only to card— the halo forms a pocket to hold Mary.

4 Cut a lamb from an old Christmas card or magazine and stick in place.

5 Knit the puppets following instructions for large size on page 6 and add bundles of wool for hair and beard.
Angel White body, pale pink face, yellow hair, blue eyes, red mouth.
Joseph Brown or drab body, fawn face, black hair, beard and eyes.
Mary Blue body, pale pink face, brown hair, brown eyes, red mouth and nose.
Stick halos to backs of heads and wings to angel.

6 Slip Mary into the pocket. Fix Joseph and the angel in place with Velcro.

7 Mount card in the usual way (see general instructions) and add a gold or yellow cord if you wish.

8 To make a larger group you could make a really big card or panel and add the three kings from page 44 and a shepherd.

Snow Scene

A card for winter birthdays or
Christmas (see colour plate opposite
page 17).

1 Cover top part of card with
bright blue material for sky, lower
part white for snow (turning the
top raw edge of the white piece to
the back) and sticking to card all
along join. Edge three sides of the

card with braid, stuck neatly to the front.

2   Trace and cut trees in three different shades of green felt. Stick in place. Cut some bobbles from white fringing and stick in place for snowballs. (Keep the braid part after the bobbles are cut off, to use for scarves.)

3   Knit the snowman all in white except the top half of head—make this black, working as given for the large size puppets on page 6. If you have any silver Lurex thread, knit it in with the wool—it makes him look frosted. Cut a black felt brim for his hat (pattern below), ease it on to head and stitch in place where black and white sections join. Embroider eyes, nose, mouth and buttons with black wool or cut them from felt and stick in place. Add a scarf of red felt or ribbon.

4   Knit the two children as given for the large size puppets on page 6, using two different colours for bodies and pink for faces until you have knitted 6 rows in pink stocking stitch. Break off pink wool and join in colour for hat. Then:

K 2 rows, p 1 row, k 1 row. (These 4 rows form the border round hat.) Work 5 rows stocking stitch for top of hat. Finish off as usual. Sew a white bobble to top of each hat and make the scarves from the braid you kept after the bobbles were cut off.

5   Embroider blue eyes, red nose and mouth and give them curly hair in two different colours by taking looped stitches in wool or embroidery cotton to cover sides and back of head.

6   Fix the puppets to the card with snippets of Velcro.

7   Mount the card in the usual way.

HAT

BRIM

SNOWMAN

52

Tea Party

A Christmas or Birthday Card
(see colour plate opposite page 16).

1 Cover the card with plain
material or with a neat stripe
suitable for wallpaper (see general
instructions).

2 Trace and cut out chairs and
table legs in wood-grain Fablon or

Contact. Stick in place. Trace and cut out table cloth in bright felt and stick a piece of white cotton fringe to lower edge. Mark creases and folds with black ball-point pen and stick to card, leaving the centre of top of table free to a depth of

about 2 inches (5 cm.) to form a pocket for the puppets.

3 Trace and cut out cakes, plates, etc., in felt or paper, mark rims of beakers, edges of cakes with black ball-point pen. Stick in place. (The beakers stuck half on table and half on card help to strengthen edges of pocket.) If for a birthday, cut as many candles as you need from white postcard, paint orange flame and stick in place.

4 Cut a picture from a magazine or postcard, draw a black frame, stick a piece of cotton to back with adhesive tape to hang it up by. Stick picture to card then push a brass-headed paper fastener through card for hanger.

5 Knit the puppets as given for the large size on page 6, giving them pink faces and different coloured dresses and hair. Embroider red nose and mouth and give one blue and one brown eyes. Make one with pigtails as given for the little girl in bed on page 42, and the other with short hair—stitched on in the same way but smoothed neatly round head and stuck in place then trimmed short. Add a bow to the top of her head. Sit the two little girls on their chairs.

6 As an extra trimming you can punch two holes in side of card, thread a piece of ribbon through and tie a neat bow. Mount card in the usual way.

Father Christmas Goes Down The Chimney

See colour plate opposite page 17.

1 Cover top of card with dark blue material. Stick yellow moon in place.

2 Cut a piece of thin card for chimney, slightly larger than picture. Paint bricks. Score and fold to make sides, and again to fold round back. Stick. Cut away surplus corners and fold bottom to make base. Stick to card by edge.

3 Stick cotton wool snow to top, paint with gum and sprinkle with glitter if you wish.

4 Mount picture on red card base (see general instructions).

A full-length view of Father Christmas is shown on page 42.

5 Knit Father Christmas as given for the large puppets on page 6. Work the first two rows of his body in double-knit white wool and garter stitch for the fur edging then change to red wool for the robe and knit a black stripe (2 rows) half way up for his belt. Use pink wool for his face. Embroider red nose, black eyes and white brows.

6 *Beard* Using double white wool, cast on 8 stitches. K 1 row. Work in garter stitch throughout to give it a rough appearance. K 2 tog at beginning of every row until 1 stitch remains. Fasten off. Sew to face.

7 *Hood* Cast on 16 stitches in double white wool for fur trimming. K 1 row. Change to red and work 10 rows in stocking stitch. Cast off. Fold hood in half and join cast-off edges on wrong side to make centre back seam. Gather round neck edge—put on to head, pull up gathers to fit and stitch in place all round neck and front fur edging. Make a tiny sack from a piece of scrim or tailor's canvas. Stuff with tissue paper and sew to back.

Put Father Christmas into the chimney.

'Knitting Guards' and Finger Puppets Combined

Finger puppets make enchanting 'guards' to prevent the stitches slipping off your knitting needles when you put the work away.

You can use any of the puppet designs given here and slipped over a pair of knitting needles they would be a very unusual present. Miniature or medium size puppets are best and as you can see, I chose the soldiers—because they are 'Guards'. When you have made your puppets, take two thimbles, put a little adhesive on to the tip of each and push one up into each puppet as far as it will go. Sew a hook to the back of each puppet as shown for the Punch and Judy figures on page 74. Cut a piece of round elastic the appropriate length and tie a loop in each end. When the toys are not in use as puppets, hook one end of the elastic to the back of each and slip

them over the ends of your knitting needles. The thimbles stop the needles poking through the puppets and will not be in the way when you are playing with the Guards— merely serving as extra grips.

56

A Blackbird

No party is complete without a small present for each guest to take home but it can be quite a headache finding something original yet inexpensive. Finger puppets can well be the answer!

'Four and twenty blackbirds baked in a pie' make an exciting centre piece for a party table—after tea everyone takes one or two birds home! Bake the pie with a filling of bread crusts, making the top crust thick and firm. When cold, gently remove the crust by slipping a sharp knife round under the edge —give the bread to the birds, wash up the dish, fill it with knitted blackbirds and replace crust (see colour plate opposite page 16).

You will need

Approx. 12 yards of black double knitting wool for the body and wings.
Two pipe cleaners for the legs.
Fine yellow wool or cotton to bind legs.
Scraps of yellow, black and white felt for eyes and beak.

How to make him

1 Wings Cast on 8 stitches.
1st row: k.
2nd row: k 2 tog, k to end.
Repeat these two rows until 1 stitch remains. Fasten off. Knit another wing in the same way. Place on one side.

2 Body Cast on 22 stitches.
1st row: k.
2nd row: k 2 tog, k, until last 2 stitches. K 2 tog.
Repeat last two rows until 14 stitches remain.
K 28 rows.
Finish off and make head as shown by Fig 1 on page 7.

3 Tail The sticking-out piece at the back is for his tail. Oversew the base of this together—then stab stitch from the bottom upwards, joining the two sides together and leaving a tube as for the people puppets (Fig 12).

4 Eye Stick a white felt eye and black felt pupil to each side of head, tracing the pattern from Fig 12.

5 Beak Cut a yellow felt beak as pattern. Fold in half at centre (broken line on pattern) and spreading a little adhesive along this line with a cocktail stick, fold and pinch together so that it remains folded. Stick edge of fold securely to front of head (Fig 12).

6 *Sew on wings* pointing upwards at a saucy angle, shown by broken lines on Fig 12.

to front of puppet by the top bent piece only and catch the two inner claws together at the tip.

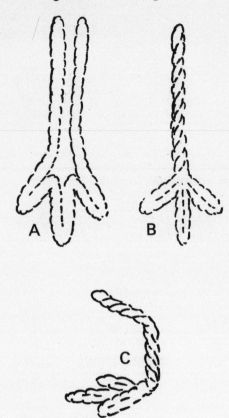

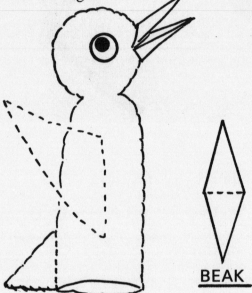

Fig 12 Attaching wing.

BEAK

Fig 13 Making the legs.

7 *Legs* Fold each pipe cleaner as Fig 13 A. Pinch the folds (claws) together and twist the straight ends to make leg (B). Bend to shape (C). Either bind tightly with fine yellow wool or embroidery cotton, fastening off very securely and dipping ends of claws and top of leg in clear gum or nail varnish for added security, or paint over the pipe cleaner with thick yellow poster paint and allow to dry.

8 *Finishing off* Sew legs securely

This puppet will stand firmly by himself as well as fitting on your finger.

Try knitting him in 'impossible' gay colours—see colour plate, opposite page 32, in which several are shown perched on the tree.

A Rooster

This is a wonderful way to use up *very* short lengths of bright coloured wools (see colour plate opposite page 32).

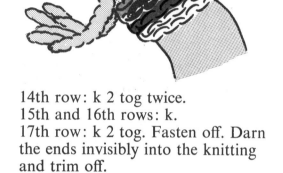

You will need

Odd lengths of red, blue, purple and green double knitting wool for feathers.
White, black or brown double knitting wool for body.
Two pipe cleaners for legs.
Fine yellow wool or cotton to bind legs.
Scraps of red, black, yellow and white felt for eyes, comb, wattles and beak.

How to make him

1 Wings Cast on 8 stitches using red wool.
1st and 2nd rows: k. Break off red wool and join in blue.
3rd and 4th rows: k. Break off blue wool and join in purple.
5th and 6th rows: k. Break off purple wool and join in green.
7th row: k.
8th row: k 2 tog, k to last 2 sts. K 2 tog. Break off green wool and join in white.
9th and 10th rows: k.
11th row: k 2 tog, k 2, k 2 tog.
12th and 13th rows: k.

14th row: k 2 tog twice.
15th and 16th rows: k.
17th row: k 2 tog. Fasten off. Darn the ends invisibly into the knitting and trim off.

2 Body Cast on 22 stitches.
1st row: k.
2nd row: k 2 tog, k to end, k 2 tog. Break off white wool leaving an end several inches long.
3rd row: Join in red wool, knotting it together with white and again leaving a long end hanging. (These long ends will eventually form the tail feathers.) K to end.
4th row: k 2 tog, k to end. Break off red wool, leaving long end.
5th row: join in blue wool, leaving long end. K to end.
6th row: k 2 tog, k to end. Break off blue wool leaving long end.
7th row: join in purple wool leaving long end. K to end.

8th row: k 2 tog, k to end. Break off purple wool leaving long end.
9th row: join in green wool leaving long end. K to end.
10th row: k 2 tog, k to end. Break off green wool leaving long end. (14 stitches.)
11th row: join in white wool. K 28 rows. (The piece now looks like Fig 14.)
Finish off and make head as shown by Fig 1 on page 7, but leave all the long ends (feathers) hanging.

3   *Tail*   Look at pictures and trim tail 'feathers' to shape, then work as given for blackbird, page 56, No 3.

4   *Eye* } Work as for blackbird,
5   *Beak* } page 56, Nos 4 and 5.

6   *Comb and wattles*   Trace these from the picture, cut out in red felt and stitch in place.

7   *Sew on wings*   Looking at picture for position, catch the two tips together at centre back over tail.

8   *Legs*   Make and attach as given for blackbird, page 57, No 7.

Like the blackbird, the rooster will stand firmly alone as well as fitting on to your finger. You might like to add him to the Easter card on page 60–61, as father to the family in the nest.

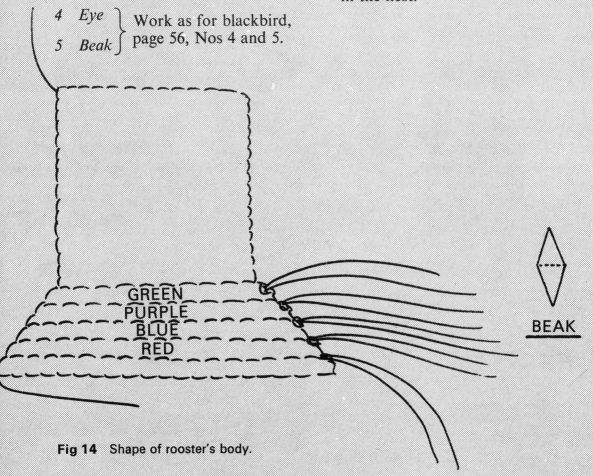

Fig 14 Shape of rooster's body.

GREEN PURPLE BLUE RED

BEAK

A Hen and Chickens

An Easter card holding three or four puppets.

You will need

Scraps of yellow and white wool for the bodies.

Red, yellow, orange and black felt for beaks, eyes and comb, and sun.

How to make them

1 The birds Using yellow wool for the chicks and white for the hen, knit and make up the puppets as given for the medium size on page 6, but work in garter stitch throughout.

2 Wings Knit a pair of wings for each bird as given for the blackbird on page 56, No 1. Sew in place, sticking up at a saucy angle.

3 Trace and cut out beaks—orange for the chicks and yellow for the hen. Fix in place as given for the blackbird on page 56. Trace and cut out comb in red felt, eyes in black. Stick all in place.

4 The card (See general instructions.) Cover with any suitable material.

5 Nest pocket Cut a matching strip of material about 8 inches × 3½ inches (20 × 9 cm.). Stick back a ½-inch (1-cm.) turning along one long (top) and one short edge, leave the other two raw. Take a hank of bass and lay it *along* the material. Machine *across* near the hemmed short end of pocket. Take a large pleat or fold in bass then stitch across again. Repeat this twice more so that the pocket is completely covered. Cut off surplus bass. Stick pocket to card, folding the raw short and long edges to back and sticking, then stick the other short edge to front of card. See that the top of pocket is loose and stands away from card a little to allow for the chicks. Cut through loops of bass.

6 Back three edges of card with a ric-rac edging.

7 Mount the picture on bright yellow card (see general instructions).

If you wish, you can tuck a few tiny Easter eggs into the pocket with the birds.

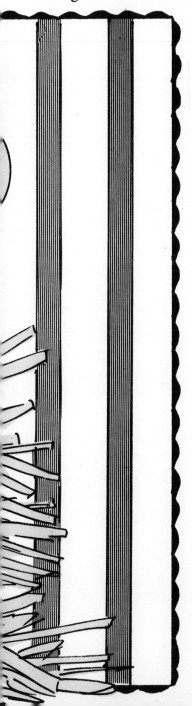

BEAK

A Parrot

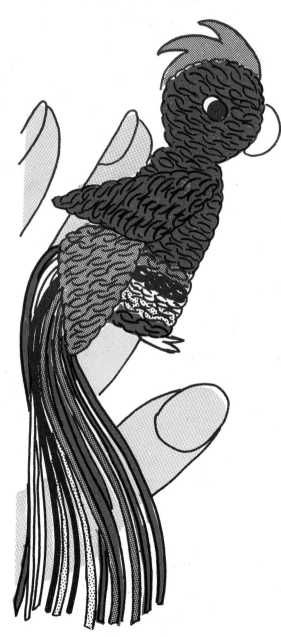

FOOT

These quickly made, gay little birds form an attractive party centre-piece if knitted in various colours and perched on a tree (see colour plate opposite page 32). After tea they become the take-home presents.

You will need

Scraps of gay coloured wool. (Original was red with blue, green, yellow and purple tail—yellow and blue also looks good.)
Scraps of yellow felt for beak and feet. Red and green for crest. Black and white for eyes.

How to make him

1 Body Work exactly as given for the rooster on page 58 (No 2), using different coloured wool and leaving extra long tail 'feathers' hanging.

2 Trace eyes, crest and beak from picture, and stick in place. Copydex smeared carefully along the edge of crest and beak with a cocktail stick will keep these pieces firmly in place, if you hold them for a few minutes until set. Look at picture and trim tail.

3 Wings Following the instructions for the blackbird on page 56 (No 1), knit two red and two green wings. Stitch a green wing to each red wing, then stitch to body, following the picture for position.

4 Trace feet from this page (one piece only—cut it out in yellow felt and stick firmly to lower edge of front of body.

A 'Puppet Pocket' Sweater for the Very Young

This polo-necked sweater has two pockets which are boats, large enough to hold four puppets between them (see colour plate opposite page 17).

To fit chest 24 (26) inches.

Materials

5 or 6 ounces Blue 4-ply knitting yarn for the main part (sea) according to the type of yarn you choose.
1 ounce White 4-ply knitting yarn for the sails and waves.
1 ounce Brown 4-ply knitting yarn for the boat and mast.
Scrap of red or yellow 4-ply knitting yarn for the pennant.
Pair No. 12 and No. 10 needles (U.S.A. 1 and 3).
A set of four No. 12 and No. 10 needles with a point at both ends.

How to check tension

Take No. 10 needles and cast on 14 stitches. Work 18 rows stocking stitch. Cast off and press lightly. This should measure 2 inches square.

If square bigger try a size finer needle.

If square smaller try a size coarser needle.

If you alter needles—corresponding alterations must be made to needles throughout.

Abbreviations

k—knit, p—purl, st—stitch, st st—stocking stitch, sl—slip, psso—pass slip stitch over, tog—together, tbl—through back of loops, inc–increase by working into stitch twice, dec—decrease by working 2 stitches together, alt—alternate, rep—repeat.

N.B. When working pattern strand yarn not in use loosely across back of work, over not more than 3 sts at a time and preferably every st to keep work elastic.

The finished work will be smoother if two separate lots of yarn are used—one for each boat. This avoids carrying the yarn across the large plain blue area between them.

Back

With No. 12 needles and blue yarn cast on 90 (106) sts.
1st row: k 1 tbl, p 1. Rep to end of row.
2nd row: k 1, p 1 tbl. Rep to end of row.
Repeat these 2 rows 5 times more **.
Change to No. 10 needles.
Continue in st st until work measures 10 (12) inches (adjust length here).

Shape raglan
Cast off 3 sts at beginning of next two rows.
1st row: k 2, sl 1, k 1, psso, k to last 4 sts, k 2 tog, k 2.
2nd row: p.

Repeat these two rows until 30 (40) sts remain.
Next row: p 2, p 2 tog, p to last 4 sts, p 2 tog tbl, p 2.
Next row: as 1st row.

2nd size only
Repeat last two rows until 28 sts remain.

Both sizes
P one row.
Slip remaining 26 (28) sts onto a length of yarn.

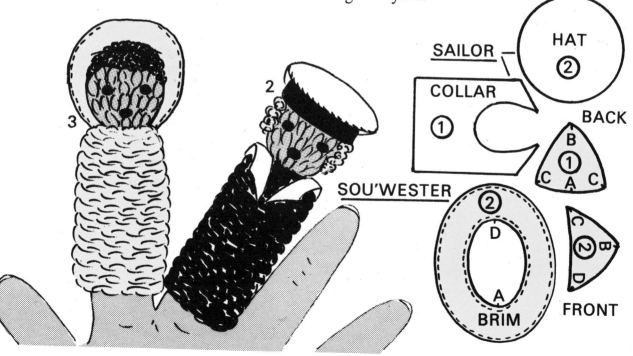

Pocket linings (2)

With blue yarn cast on 24 sts on
No. 10 needles and work 12 rows
in st st. Leave sts on a spare needle.

Front

(Pattern for boat is chart on Fig 15.)

Fig 15.

Work as back to **.
Change to No. 10 needles.
Work 2 rows st st.
Next row: k 7 (11), work 1st row
of first boat pattern, k 12 (20), work
1st row of second boat pattern, k 5
(9).
Next row: p 5 (9), work 2nd row
of pattern, p 12 (20), work 2nd
row of pattern, p 7 (11).
Work rows 3 to 16 on chart as
above, knitting and purling in blue
yarn each side of and between the
boats.
Next row: k 10 (14), slip next 24 sts
onto length of yarn, k 24 sts across
one pocket lining, k 24 (32), slip
24 sts onto length of yarn, k 24 sts
across second pocket lining, k 10
(14).
Next row: p.
Work 17 to 56 rows on chart as
above, knitting and purling in blue
yarn each side of and between the
boats, as necessary.
Work in st st in blue until work
measures 10 (12) ins.

Shape raglans
Cast off 3 sts at beginning of next
two rows.
Work 1st and 2nd rows as on back
until 52 (60) sts remain, ending
with a 2nd row.

Shape neck
Next row: k 2, sl 1, k 1, psso, k 16
(20), turn and leave remaining sts
on length of yarn.
Continue with 19 sts on needle as
follows:
Dec 1 st on raglan edge every
alternate row as before while at the
same time dec 1 st at neck edge on

every alt row until 9 (11) sts remain.
Continue decreasing at raglan edge
only as before until 4 (8) sts remain.

2nd size only
1st row: p to last 4 sts, p 2 tog tbl,
p 2.
2nd row: k 1, sl 1, k 1, psso, k to
end.
Repeat last 2 rows once more.

All sizes
Next row: p 2 tog tbl, p 2.
Next row: k 1, sl 1, k 1, psso.
Next row: p.
K 2 tog and fasten off.
Leave centre 12 sts on length of
yarn.
With right side facing, join yarn to
remaining sts and knit up to match
first side, reversing shapings.

N.B.   p 2 tog will replace p 2 tog
tbl at raglan shaping.

Pocket tops

Slip pocket top stitches on to
No. 12 needle and using brown
yarn k 1 row, inc 4 times evenly
across row.
Work 4 rows in k 1 tbl, p 1 rib.
Using No. 10 needles cast off in rib.

N.B.   This top looks attractive if
one or two stripes to match the
pennant are knitted in.

Sleeves

With No. 12 needles cast on 44 (52)
sts.

1st row: k 1 tbl, p 1, rep to end of
row.
2nd row: k 1, p 1 tbl, rep to end of
row.
Repeat these two rows 7 times more.
Change to No. 10 needles.
Work in st st, inc 1 st at each end
of 5th and every following 6th row
until there are 60 (72) sts then every
8th row until there are 66 (82) sts.

Continue straight until sleeve seam
measures 11 (13) inches ending with
p row (adjust length here).

Shape raglan
Cast off 3 sts at beginning of next
two rows.
1st row: k 2, sl 1, k 1, psso, k to
last 4 sts, k 2 tog, k 2.
2nd row: p.

1st size only
3rd row: k.
4th row: p.
Repeat rows 1 to 4 once more
(56 sts).

Both sizes
Rep 1st and 2nd rows until 8 (12)
sts remain.

2nd size only
Next row: p 2, p 2 tog, p to last
4 sts, p 2 tog tbl, p 2.
Next row: as 3rd row.

Both sizes
Work 1 row.
Slip sts onto length of yarn.

To make up and polo collar

Press pieces avoiding ribbing. Using

a fine back stitch, join raglan seams.
With set of No. 12 needles, k 8
sleeve sts, k up 17 (20) sts down
left side of neck, k across 12 sts at
centre front, k up 17 (20) sts up
right side of neck, k 8 sleeve sts,
k 26 (28) across back (88 (96) sts).
Work in k 1 tbl, p 1 rib for 2 inches.
Change to set of No. 10 needles
and k 1, p 1 tbl rib until collar
measures 4½ inches.
Cast off loosely in rib.
Using flat seam for ribbing and
back stitch for remainder, join side
and sleeve seams.
Slip-stitch pocket linings into
position.
Sew pocket-tops into position.
Press seam.

The pocket boats are now ready to
hold their finger puppet crews.
Each boat will hold one or two
little men and four characters are
given here, so choose which you
prefer or make one of each!

A Sailor
A Yachtsman in Oil-Skins
A Deep Sea Fisherman
A Pirate

All the puppets are made to the
medium size pattern on page 6, but
the body parts were knitted in
double knitting wool.

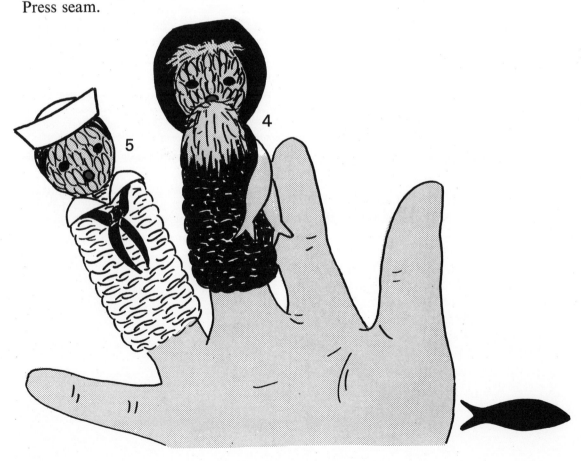

The Pocket Puppets

1   The Pirate   (Illustration page 63.)
Lower half of body black for trousers, top half red/white or blue/white stripe for shirt. Pink or fawn face. Embroider one black eye, red mouth, stick on black felt eye patch. Make grey looped wool or stranded cotton stitches round chin and up sides of face for beard and hair. Sew two small rings in place for ear-rings. (Bolt rings or links from an old necklace?) Stitch a scrap of red/white spotted cotton material round the head, tying or stitching at back.

2   British sailor   (Illustration p. 64.)
Navy blue body for tunic and trousers. Pink or fawn face. Embroider blue eyes, red mouth. Make yellow or brown looped wool or stranded cotton stitches over sides and back of head for hair. Trace and cut out collar and hat in white felt, cut another hat circle in thin card. Stick collar in place. Place the card hat piece between the two felt pieces and oversew all round the edge. Stick firmly to top of head. Cut a narrow strip of navy felt, stick round head under hat with two fish-tail ends sticking out at back. (You could easily turn him into an American sailor—ideas for this are given in the picture on page 67 (No. 5).)

3   Yachtsman   (Illustration p. 64.)
Yellow body for oilskins, pink face. Embroider blue eyes, red mouth. Make brown looped wool or stranded cotton stitches on top of front of head for hair. Cut out the pieces for the sou'wester in yellow felt. Stab stitch the two brim pieces neatly together all round outside and inside edges, as shown by broken lines on pattern. On the wrong side join two front sections B–D (centre front seam) then join on the back section C–B–C. Oversew this piece to brim, matching D's and A's. Press and stretch it well on to yachtsman's head, sticking firmly in place. Turn up front brim and stick it to crown of hat.

4   Deep sea fisherman   (Illustration page 67.)
Make exactly as given for yachtsman but use black wool for body and black felt for hat. Stick scraps of grey fur fabric (or wool) in place for hair and beard. Cut out one or two fish in grey felt, stitch to shoulder by mouth ends in a little bundle. Arrange down side of body and stick in place.

A Hula-Hooping Clown

See colour plate opposite page 16.

You will need

Two circles cut from an old pair of tights, the size of Tom Thumb's head, page 89.
A scrap of gay cotton material 5 inches long × 3 inches deep (12 × 7 cm.) for tunic.
A scrap of round elastic.
Approximately 8 inches (20 cm.) white tape for ruff, 1 inch (2·5 cm.) wide.
Three black bobbles for hair.
Scraps of red and white felt for features.

How to make him

1　Make head as given for Thumbelina, page 88, No 1, stuffing it very full to make it larger.

2　Fold tunic piece in half and on the wrong side join the 3-inch ends (centre back seam). Gather along top edge, pull up and fasten off (neck end). Make a narrow hem round lower edge and insert a piece of round elastic to fit finger. Turn tunic right side out. Sew gathered top to base of head (gathers on head at centre back).

3　Stick three black bobbles round back of head for hair, covering gathers. Trace features from picture and cut out in felt, white eye and mouth make-up, red nose and mouth. Stick in place. Mark eye crosses with black felt pen.

4　Make ruff as given for Punch, page 74, No 6.

Use the clown on your forefinger—with a little practice you will be able to make him use a large bangle or a ring cut from the edge of a plastic container as a hula-hoop. The larger the hoop the easier it is to spin (the ideal size seems to be 4 inches (10 cm.) diameter).

A Punch and Judy Show

General instructions

Punch and Judy shows vary, as do the number of characters appearing in the cast. Only the basic characters are given here as there is a limit to what one can do with one's fingers! In order to make the show lively Punch remains in sight most of the time and the other characters come and go, popping up and down at the appropriate moment. It is best to keep Punch on the forefinger of your right hand and one other character on the forefinger of your left.

The traditional Punch voice is made with a 'swazzle'. This is a piece of tape between two pieces of metal and is held in the performer's mouth. This needs practice and training to perfect—don't try it, you might swallow part of the swazzle! If you could get a friend to speak through a comb and paper it would give a very realistic effect. If you want to find out more about the characters and get ideas for the story read *Punch and Judy* by George Speaight (Studio Vista).

The booth

A booth made from a large shoe box 13 inches long × 6½ inches wide × 4¼ inches deep (33 × 16·5 × 10·5 cm.) is shown on the front and back cover of this book. Discard the box lid and look at the cover for guidance.

1 With a sharp knife cut out the end 4 inches (10 cm.) of base. Stand box on end.

2 Slit down a further 1 inch (2·5 cm.) at each side of this opening and bend forward for the 'playboard'. Strengthen this by sticking another piece of cardboard on the top and bottom of it.

3 Unless your box is very strong indeed, line it out with pieces of cardboard cut from other odd boxes, sticking them firmly in place, so that your booth is quite rigid.

4 Cover the outside with narrow red/white striped cotton material and the inside with felt of your choice. Cover the playboard top and bottom with fawn or grey felt, sticking everything firmly in place.

5 Fold a strip of red/white striped material double and stick round edge of playboard. Stick a similar piece across top—in both cases turning in the raw edges at sides.

6 Sew rings or pieces of chain inside back, by which to hang up the puppets. It is then easy to slip your fingers into them as needed.

The easiest way to use the booth is to stand it close to the back edge of a table and sit on a chair behind it. A lot of practice is needed to give

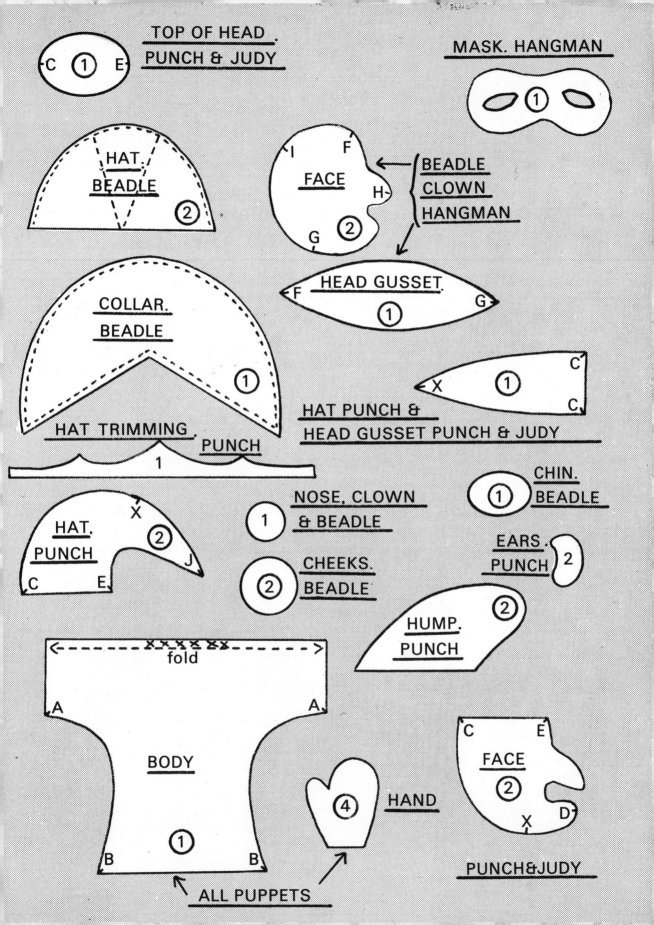

TOP OF HEAD.
PUNCH & JUDY

C 1 E

MASK. HANGMAN

1

HAT.
BEADLE
2

FACE
2

I F
H
G

← BEADLE
CLOWN
HANGMAN

HEAD GUSSET.
1

F G

COLLAR.
BEADLE
1

HAT PUNCH &
HEAD GUSSET PUNCH & JUDY

X 1 C
C

HAT TRIMMING
PUNCH
1

HAT.
PUNCH
C E
X
2
J

NOSE, CLOWN
& BEADLE
1

CHEEKS.
BEADLE
2

CHIN.
1 BEADLE

EARS.
PUNCH 2

HUMP.
PUNCH
2

BODY
1

fold
A A
B B

HAND
4

FACE
2
C E
X D

PUNCH & JUDY

ALL PUPPETS

a polished performance and the best way to do this is to work opposite a mirror so that you can see the effect you are making and correct your faults as they arise.

Head for Punch and Judy

1 Cut out the face, head gusset and top of head in flesh pink felt (4 pieces) patterns page 71.

2 On the right side oversew the two face pieces together E–D–X. Insert gusset stitching C–X–C. Stuff firmly, paying particular attention to pointed chin and nose by pushing tiny pieces of kapok into the tips with a cocktail stick.

3 Oversew top of head in place, matching C's and E's, pushing more stuffing inside (to make the head very firm) as you work. Place on one side.

Head for beadle, clown and hangman

1 Cut out the face and head gusset in flesh pink felt, patterns page 71 (3 pieces).

2 On the right side neatly oversew the two face pieces together all round nose and chin F–H–G. Insert head gusset, oversewing F–G first to one face piece then to the other, leaving a small opening I–F for stuffing on one side. Stuff very firmly paying particular attention to nose and chin. Sew up opening. Place on one side.

Finger grip

1 Using a needle stuck into a cork (Fig 16), make two holes in the top of a small plastic thimble (Fig 17 A). Make the needle red hot by holding it in a candle flame so that it slides easily through the plastic.

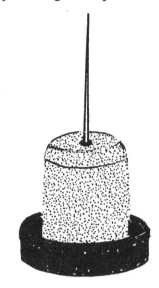

Fig 16 Needle stuck into cork.

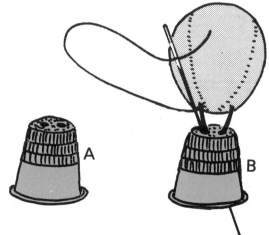

Fig 17 Sewing head to thimble.

2 Stitch the base of head to the thimble, using strong thread and working through the holes (B).

3 Twist a pipe cleaner for stiffening arms round thimble (Fig 18), securing it with Copydex. Place on one side.

and pipe cleaner down into body, easing cleaners out at sleeve ends (Fig 19).

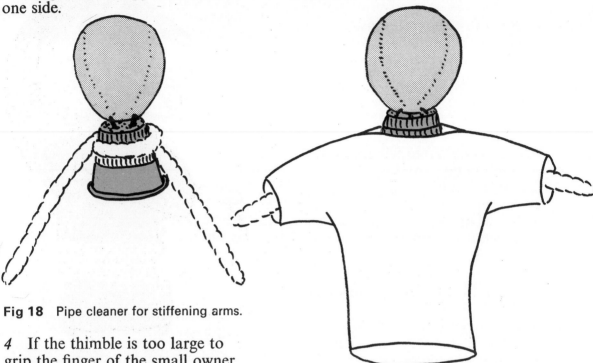

Fig 18 Pipe cleaner for stiffening arms.

4 If the thimble is too large to grip the finger of the small owner firmly, make it smaller by sticking layers of adhesive tape round the inside.

Fig 19 Thimble in position inside body.

Body for all main characters

1 Cut out piece in appropriate coloured felt, also the hands (patterns page 71).

2 Fold body as shown on pattern and on the wrong side oversew sides together A–B. Turn right side out.

3 Cut a slit just large enough for the base of a thimble to slip through where marked by XXXX on pattern then push prepared thimble

4 Place a little adhesive on top of thimble and push head down on to it. Stitch body to head, working round edge of slit. Place the hands together in pairs. Oversew together all round except short, straight edge. Stuff, pushing filling down into thumb with a cocktail stick. Push hands on to ends of pipe cleaner arm stiffeners (thumb uppermost), easing them well on. Gather edge of sleeves and stitch firmly to hands. Sew a large hook upside down to centre back at bottom by which to hang your puppet inside the booth in the traditional manner.

Punch

Punch, of course, is a must—always the central character and much loved hero of the drama as he wields his stick.

You will need

A basic body in red felt complete with head and hands.
Scraps of red felt for mouth, hat and hump.
Scraps of black, white, yellow and green felt for features and trimmings.
Black wool for hair.
Approximately 8 inches (20 cm.) of 1-inch (2.5-cm.) wide white tape or ribbon for ruff.
A tiny bell or bead for hat.
Three large, round yellow buttons (or beads) for tunic.
A small piece of strong stick.

How to make him (Look at picture on cover for front view.)

1 Cut out hat, gusset, hump, ears and hat trimming (8 pieces), patterns page 71.

2 On the wrong side oversew two pieces of hump together all round curved edge. Stuff firmly. Place open end flat against top part of back and ladder stitch in place working all round.

3 Embroider black wool hair, using long straight stitches and covering back and sides of head.

4 Oversew two hat pieces together E–J–X, insert gusset C–X–C. Stuff very firmly and sew to head, point forwards. Stick bead to point.

5 Cut out and stick on red, smiling mouth, white eyes, black pupils. Stick on ears. Tint nose, chin, cheeks and edges of ears with red water-colour and when dry mark brows with black felt pen.

6 Using red and black felt pens mark coloured stripes round edges of ribbon for ruff. Join short ends, gather up and sew to neck.

7 Sew three round, yellow buttons (or beads) to front of tunic and stitch a piece of strong stick in crook of right arm.

Clown

Punch always has a cheerful companion who is the only character not to be killed. He helps get rid of the hangman's corpse and constantly confuses and teases Punch. Sometimes he is Scaramouche and sometimes Joey the clown.

You will need

A basic body in white felt complete with hands and face.
Scrap of white ribbon and trimming for ruff approximately 8 inches (20 cm.) × 1 inch (2·5 cm.) wide.
Three large black bobbles for hair and four small coloured ones for pom-pons.
Red, black and white felt for features.
Black wool for eyes and back hair.

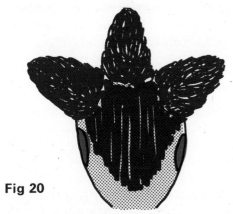

Fig 20

How to make him

1 Cut out the false nose in red felt, pattern, page 71 (1 piece).
2 Embroider back hair using black wool and long stitches reaching well up to top of head. With sharp scissors trim the three black bobbles to pointed cones for hair peaks and stick firmly to head in positions shown, pressing well down (Fig 20).

3 *Gather round edge of false nose, pull up gathers and stitch to centre of face over the top of protruding nose. Stuff a little if necessary to make a firm knob.* Taking shapes from picture, cut out white eye and mouth make-up, black eyebrows, red mouth and spots. Stick all to face. Embroider eye crosses with black wool.

4 Join the short ends of the piece of white ribbon for ruff. Stick a narrow braid (or wool) trimming round edge, gather up and stitch round neck. Finish with yellow pom-pons on sleeves and tunic.

Judy

Judy, Punch's wife, with the same distorted features under her traditional white mob cap, constantly falls the victim of her husband's stick and has mild hysterics when he ill-treats her baby.

You will need

A basic body in blue (or some suitable colour) complete with head and hands.
Scraps of white, red, black and blue felt for collar, cuffs, features, and hat trimming.
7 inches (18 cm.) broderie anglaise 1¾ inches (4·5 cm.) wide for mob cap.
Brown wool for hair.

How to make her

1   Look at picture on cover for front view. Using flesh-coloured thread, stitch a small bundle of brown wool to centre front of head for hair (stitches are the parting). Spread a little adhesive to head and smooth hair neatly sideways and backwards, sticking in place. Cut off ends which will be hidden under mob cap.

2   Stick red, smiling mouth, white eyes, black pupils in place. Tint chin, nose and cheeks with red water-colour and when dry, mark brows with brown felt pen.

3   Stick a ½-inch (1-cm.) wide strip of white felt round neck for collar, joining under chin and cutting away to points each side (like a shirt collar). Stick very narrow strips round wrists for cuffs.

4   On the wrong side join short ends of broderie anglaise for cap. Gather along straight edge and pull up (centre back). Turn right side out. Run a gathering thread all round approximately ¾ inch (2 cm.) in from fancy edge. Put on head and pull up to fit. Stitch to head all round gathers. Finish with a strip of blue felt. Give Judy her baby to hold.

The Crocodile

A crocodile always appears to snap and fight with Punch and usually ends by swallowing his stick or a string of sausages!

You will need

A green plastic clip clothes peg (or as original—a wooden one with green felt stuck to outside).
Scraps of red felt for nostrils.
Scraps of white postcard or plastic for teeth.

1 Stick two red nostrils to top of open end.

2 Cut and stick in place four sets of white zig-zag teeth.

3 Sew a hook to base, well out of the way of where fingers will hold the ends of peg to open and shut jaws. (N.B. The spring closely resembles an eye.) If a plastic peg is used the hook must of course be omitted.

The Baby

The baby is carried by Judy and gets on Punch's nerves so much that he twirls it round and round on his stick and eventually throws it out of the window, 'What a pity— What a pity.'

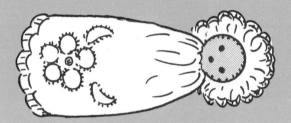

You will need

Scraps of flesh felt for face.
Scraps of broderie anglaise 2 inches wide (5 cm.) × 3 inches long (7·5 cm.) for dress and ¾ inch wide (2 cm.) × 2 inches long (5 cm.) for bonnet.

1 Cut two circles of flesh felt the size of ½p piece. On the right side oversew them together all round the edge, pushing a little stuffing inside as you work. Mark blue eyes and red mouth.

2 Join the ends of the wide piece of broderie anglaise on the wrong side to make a ring for dress. Gather along top straight edge taking a tiny turning as you work. Pull up gathers and sew to face under chin.

3 Gather along straight edge of the narrow piece for bonnet. Pull up gathers (centre back). Sew to baby's head. Put her into Judy's arms.

The Beadle

The beadle represents the law, being an official of the parish, with many duties. He is really an essential character as someone must arrest Punch. Sometimes modern shows substitute a policeman.

You will need

A basic body in dark red felt complete with hands and face.
Scraps of dark red felt for collar and hat trimming.
Scraps of black felt for hat, yellow for coat 'opening'.
Scraps of flesh, blue, white and red for features.
Scraps of very narrow yellow braid for trimming (or yellow knitting wool).
White wool for hair.

How to make him

1 Cut out the hat, collar, nose, chin and cheeks (7 pieces), patterns page 71.

2 Make and attach the nose as for clown, page 75, No 3, but in flesh felt, working from *–*.
Stick a tiny red felt mouth under it.

3 Gather round cheeks and chin in a similar way. Stuff to form knobs and sew to face to give a very fat, bloated appearance. Tint nose, chin and cheeks with weak, red water-colour. Stick on white eyes, blue pupils. Stick short lengths of white wool to top of head for hair. Trim neatly.

4 Oversew curved edges of hat together on wrong side. Turn right side out. Stick a V of dark red felt to front. Stick yellow trimming in place as shown by broken lines on pattern. Smear adhesive on top of head and stick hat firmly in place.

5 Edge collar with braid and stick firmly to body (look at picture).

6 Stick an inverted V of dark yellow felt to front of body to indicate where coat parts and edge with yellow braid.

The Hangman

The hangman comes to deal with Punch when he is eventually captured. We all know the enchanting sequel when Punch pretends he cannot understand how to put his head in the noose of the gallows, so the hangman shows him how by putting his own head in and Punch pulls the rope thus hanging the hangman.

You will need

A basic body in black, complete with hands and face.
Scraps of black felt for hood and mask.
Scraps of red and white felt for features.
A few inches of string for 'rope'.

How to make him

1 Cut out the mask (pattern page 71) and hood (pattern below) —2 pieces.

2 Fold the hood in half lengthwise (fold comes on top of head) and on

Fig 21

the wrong side oversew seam A–B. Place on one side.

3 On wrong side of mask stick white felt patches to completely cover eye holes. Stick mask to face, pressing well down over nose. Mark pupils with black felt pen. Cut a curved red mouth and stick to face in cleft between nose and chin, turning downwards in a gloomy manner.

4 Spread adhesive over head and stick hood in place pulling it well on to cover top of mask. Add a few stitches here and there to bring it into the curve of neck.

5 Twist a piece of string round the top of right arm for his rope and stick or stitch securely in place.

HOOD

B   A   B

Dressed Felt Mice and Bears

These gay little felt characters need no finger grips as their slim, straight bodies keep them firmly in place. The bodies are machined and the heads for which there are two basic patterns are hand sewn (see colour plate opposite pages 16 & 17). All ten variations are shown on pages 80, 85 and 87 as bears but they can equally well be made up as mice. (Three are pictured below.) Only tiny scraps of felt and oddments of braid, etc., are needed and wisps of kapok or similar, for stuffing heads and hats.

N.B. The body is used for 'The Cow with the Crumpled Horn' and the dog on pages 94–95 and you will easily see how to use various animal heads as alternatives.

How to make them

Basic head for bears
1 Cut out the head, head gusset and ears (5 pieces) using fawn felt, patterns page 81.

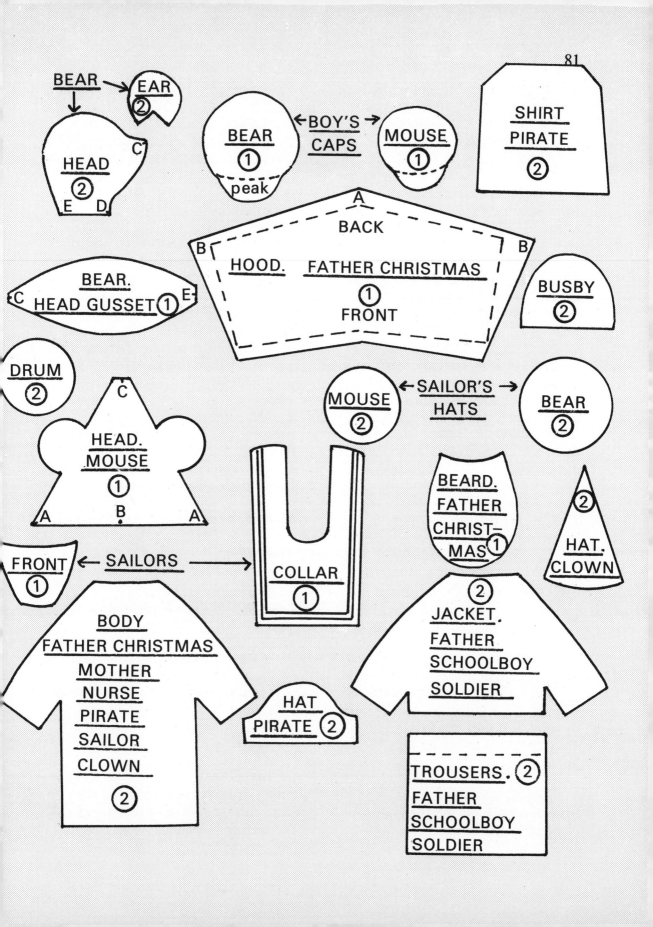

2 On the right side, stab stitch (or oversew) the head pieces to head gusset C–E. Join the two head pieces together C–D.

3 Stuff head, leaving a little at the neck end empty. Sew front centre seam to centre back and close neck across.

4 Embroider eyes or use coloured felt circles (cut with a leather punch if you have one) and black embroidered pupils. Embroider black nose and mouth.

5 Sew on ears, curving them round at an attractive angle. These look very ugly if they are too large which sometimes happens when tracing from such a small pattern. Trim away the edges to reduce the size if necessary.

Basic head for mice
1 Cut out the piece in grey felt (pattern page 81).

2 Fold head in half so that A's meet and join A–B.

3 Turn right side out.

4 Stuff firmly.

5 Stitch C to A, then join side to edge of ear. Gather round ear close to head and pull tightly. Fasten off and repeat on the other side of head.

6 To pull up ears, run a thread from the back of one through top of head to the other.

7 Embroider black eyes and nose.

8 To add whiskers, thread a length of horsehair or strong linen thread into a needle, making a knot at the end. Just before whisker enters face put a tiny spot of adhesive on to knot and pull through into head. Cut each whisker (four is a good number) to the required length.

Basic body
1 Cut out body (2 pieces) in appropriate coloured felt, pattern page 81, and two strips for hands $\frac{3}{4}$ inch $\times \frac{1}{4}$ inch (2 cm. $\times \frac{1}{2}$ cm.) in grey or fawn felt to match head.

2 Machine the two body pieces together on the right side, inserting the strips for hands folded double, into the ends of sleeves as you work. Leave neck and base open.

Mother in indoor clothes (1 and 2).

You will need
A head and basic body in any gay colour.
Piece of ribbon for apron 1½ inches × 1½ inches (4 cm. × 4 cm.).
Piece of narrow lace approximately 2½ inches (6·5 cm.) long for collar.

1 Hem ribbon at one end. Gather other end. Stitch gathered end to waist, keeping sides of body apart by inserting a ruler.

2 Insert head into neck of body, bringing body well up on to the head (about ¼ inch (½ cm.)) and sew firmly in place.

3   Join ends of lace and gather up to make frilly collar.

Mother in outdoor clothes (3).

You will need
A head and basic body in any gay colour.
4½ inches (11·5 cm.) ric-rac and a scrap of fur fabric.

1   Machine piece of ric-rac up centre front before making up body, starting at lower edge and leaving long end at neck.

2   Make body and insert head.

3   Use end of ric-rac, stitched round neck for collar.

4   Stitch scrap of fur fabric to top of head for hat.

Father (4 and 12).

You will need
A head.
Two colours of felt for jacket and trousers.
Scrap of ribbon or bias binding for scarf.

1   Cut out jacket and trousers (4 pieces). Patterns page 81.

2   Stitch a line down centre front of trousers to indicate two legs.

3   Place the jacket over trousers at broken lines and machine.

4   Machine front and back together inserting hands folded double into sleeve ends at the same time and leaving neck and base open.

5   Insert head into body and stitch.

6   Tie ribbon or binding round neck and stitch in place for scarf. (N.B. Adhesive on raw edges prevents fraying.)

Schoolboy (5).

You will need
A head.
A body made up as for father (No 4).
Scraps of gay felt for cap and badge. White for collar.
Ribbon or strip of felt for tie.

1   Cut out cap (1 piece) pattern page 81.

2   Having made body and inserted head, sew on tie. Embroider tie pin.

3   Sew on a narrow band of white felt for collar.

4   Start sewing on cap at centre front leaving peak loose—continue sewing all round edge. Finish off with school badge in front.

Red Cross nurse (6).

You will need
A head.
A basic body in blue felt.
White ribbon or tape for apron

$1\frac{1}{2}$ inches × $1\frac{1}{2}$ inches (4 cm. × 4 cm.).
A piece of $\frac{1}{2}$-inch (1·5-cm.) wide
white ribbon or tape 3 inches
(7·5 cm) long for bib and cap.
Strip of white felt $\frac{1}{4}$ inch ($\frac{1}{2}$ cm.)
wide for collar.

1 Insert head into body.

2 Cut narrow ribbon in half. Fold
one piece into three. Embroider
Red Cross in centre. Sew this to
body for bib. Make apron as for
mother and sew to body covering
lower edge of bib.

3 Fold the other narrow piece
into three for cap. Embroider Red
Cross in centre just above edge.
(Selvedges of ribbon are sides of
cap.) Sew cap to front of head, then
to back, leaving sides open to go
over ears.

4 Sew white collar round neck.

Sailor (7).

You will need
A head.
A basic body in navy blue felt.
Scraps of white felt for hat and
collar, navy for 'ribbon', black for
bow.

1 Cut out hat, collar and front
(4 pieces) patterns page 81.

2 Before making up body, machine
two double lines on both pieces to
indicate tunic and trouser legs.

3 Make body and insert head.

4 Stitch white 'front' round front
of neck.

5 Sew on collar working from
centre back forwards over white
front on both sides. Using blue
thread embroider a double line all
round outside edge of collar. (This
helps to attach the collar firmly to
body.) Finish off at front with a
small black bow.

6 In one hat piece cut a slit large
enough to push ear through.
Oversew circles together. Push one
ear inside hat and stitch firmly to
head. Sew narrow band of blue
felt round head at base of hat,
finishing at side with long ends.

Clown (8).

You will need
A head.
A basic body in any gay colour.
White ric-rac for ruff.
Five white circles for pom-pons.

1 Cut out hat (2 pieces), pattern
page 81.

2 Stitch 3 circles for pom-pons to
front of hat.

3 Insert head and finish neck with
a band of white ric-rac for a ruff.

4 Make hat by oversewing from
top point to three-quarters of the
way down each side, leaving room
for ears. Stuff hat and stitch to
head.

Pirate (9 and 13).

You will need
A head.
A basic body in any gay colour.
Black felt for hat. Bright felt for
collar.
Striped cotton material for shirt.

N.B.   No turnings are allowed on
the shirt pattern.

1   Cut out hat and shirt (4 pieces),
patterns page 81.

2   Machine shirt into position on
both body pieces before making
body up. Insert head.

3   Embroider skull and crossbones
on front of hat. Oversew pieces
together, leaving sides open for
ears. Stuff top of hat and stitch to
head, allowing ears to go inside
and stick out at sides.

4   Finish neck with narrow band
of bright felt.

Father Christmas (10).
You will need
A head.
A basic body in red felt.
Red felt for hood.
Scraps of white fur fabric.

1   Cut out hood to broken line for
mouse, full size for bear and beard
(2 pieces), pattern page 81.

2   Insert head into body.

3   Fold hood in half and machine
back seam A–B on the wrong side.
Turn right side out. Sew to head
making sure the back covers back
of head. Push ears inside (or don't

bother to make any).

4   Apply adhesive to narrow strip
of fur fabric and stick round edge
of hood, continuing round back of
neck and finishing in front.

5   A little adhesive applied to
edges of beard will prevent fraying.
When dry stitch in place and secure
to chest with adhesive.

Soldier (11).

You will need
A head.
A basic body as for father—red
top, black trousers.
Scrap of black fur fabric for busby.
Two colours of felt for drum.
Match sticks.
Scrap of coloured string.

1   Cut out busby and drum (4
pieces), patterns page 81.

2   Insert head into body finishing
neck with band of red felt.

3   Oversew two sides of busby
firmly together on the wrong side
leaving small opening on either side
for ears. Turn right side out and
sew to head pushing ears inside
and closing opening over them.

4   Oversew drum circles to $\frac{1}{4}$ inch
($\frac{1}{2}$ cm.) band for edge. Stuff drum
and finish sides with zig-zag stitches
in gay colour. Stick drum firmly to
tunic. Sew coloured string to drum
to hang round neck.

5   Spread a little adhesive on the
ends of two pieces of match stick
and push into hand loops. Stick
the sleeve ends and hands to drum.

8

9

10

11

Two Thumb Puppets

See colour plate opposite page 32.

You will need

* A thimble to fit the thumb.
* A scrap of pink stockinette (old undies?) for head.
12 inches (30 cm.) of lace 2 inches (5 cm.) wide, for dress.
2 inches (5 cm.) of yellow lampshade fringe for hair.
Scraps of very narrow ribbon for sash and hair.
* 2 pipe cleaners for limbs.
* Red and blue stranded cotton for features.
* Knob of cotton wool for head.
* Pink nail varnish for painting hands and legs.

How to make Thimble Thumbelina

1 Trace and cut out head, using pattern on page 93. Gather all round the edge. Put a knob of stuffing in centre and pull up gathers and fasten off securely.

2 Prepare thimble as shown for Punch (page 72, Fig 17 A).

3 Join short ends of lace, forming a ring. Gather along top straight edge, pull up tightly and fasten off.

4 Place prepared lace over thimble gathers on top, then attach head as shown for Punch, page 72 (Fig 17 B) stitching right through lace and thus attaching skirt at the same time. (The gathers on head should be at centre back.)

5 Run a second gathering thread round lace approximately $\frac{1}{2}$ inch (1 cm.) from head. Smear the top half of thimble with adhesive. Pull up gathers to fit thimble tightly (the waist), fasten off and press the lace above gathers to the thimble so that it sticks. Tie a narrow sash of ribbon round waist.

6 Embroider red mouth, blue eyes.

7 Smear Copydex over top of head and press the lampshade fringe round it for hair. Tie the fringe into a pony tail with a narrow ribbon.

8 Fold the pipe cleaners in two as shown by Fig 22 A and twist and press them tightly together. Bend one cleaner into a U shape and sew it inside of skirt for legs.

9 Bind the other cleaner with a scrap of narrow lace (sleeves) except for a tiny piece at each end (hands). Bend this to a U shape and sew to centre back just above sash.

10 Bend up hands and feet and paint with pink nail varnish.

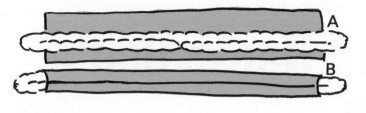

Fig 22

You will need

The items marked * for Thimble-Thumbelina.
Some scraps of white or coloured stockinette (part of old socks or Tee shirt?).
Scrap of brown felt for hair.

HAIR —

How to make Tom Thimble-thumb

1 Make head and embroider features as given for Thumbelina.

2 Prepare thimble as given for Punch (page 72, Fig 17 A) making two holes on top.

3 Cut a circle of stockinette for the body the same size as head. Lay it on top of thimble and stitch head to thimble working right through the stockinette and holes in thimble.

4 Smear thimble with adhesive and press stockinette well down onto it, pleating and pressing all round to make the body. Trim lower edge. Cut hair from brown felt, smear one side with adhesive, place on head and press well in place.

5 Fold pipe cleaners double as Fig 22 A. Press well together. Lay each one on a narrow strip of stockinette well smeared with adhesive (A). (The stockinette should be a little shorter than cleaners, to allow hands and feet to protrude at each end.) Roll stockinette tightly round cleaners and press well so that it sticks (B). Bend to U shape and stick one firmly to top and one to bottom for arms and legs. Adjust hands and feet and paint with pink nail varnish.

This is the House that Jack Built

I have included this wall-hanging, which holds ten puppets—one for each finger—in an attempt to show how the characters given in other parts of the book may be altered and adapted for many purposes and the various types mixed quite happily. First make the house, following the picture on pages 94–95.

This is the house that Jack built

1 Cut out the basic shape in medium gauge cardboard. (You need it as thick as possible, bearing in mind that you will have to cut out the windows.)

2 Stick a piece of grey or white felt over the card for the house and a piece of red felt or textured tweed on top of this for the roof, turning the edges to the back and sticking.

3 Cut out the windows (not the door) and discard the pieces. (Cut them a little longer than shown, so that the window boxes will cover lower edges.) Cut out the window in roof. (A knife may help here.)

4 Cut white postcard for window boxes and stick a piece of flowered braid across the top of each for flowers, turning the raw ends to the back behind postcard. Write a name on each window box and stick one to each window, except the one in roof.

5 Turn picture to wrong side and stick small pieces of lace in place for curtains.

6 Cut out and stick on a bright coloured door, with a white card triangle over it. Write Jack on this. Stick on a door frame and arch of wood-grain Fablon or Contact, or dark coloured felt.

7 Fix a ring to back with a piece of adhesive tape so that you can hang the picture up and stick a slice cut from a cork to each corner (also at the back) to keep it slightly away from the wall and allow room for the puppets' bodies.

This is the malt . . . that lay in the house that Jack built

Cut out a sack shape from a piece of scrim or similar coarse material and stick in place by the door. Add a tiny white paper label and write 'malt' on it.

*   *   *   *

This is how I made the puppets, but do try to use your own ideas. (It is of course unavoidable that the characters are out of proportion, but in nursery-rhyme land, this doesn't matter at all.)

Jack is fixed to the door with Velcro (see page 8). The cock merely tucks into the roof window, his head and wattles keeping him in place. The other puppets have one or two small hooks sewn to the back of their heads and are hung on to the lace curtains!

**This is the rat
That ate the malt . . .**

To make the rat cut out the shape (pattern page 93) in grey velvet or any suitable material. Fold it in half as shown and on the wrong side join seam A–B. Turning a narrow hem all round narrow curved edge and insert a piece of round elastic so that the wide end of rat grips finger. Turn right side out. Embroider black nose and eyes and insert whiskers (look at pages 94–95). Cut out two felt ears, fold in half, oversew base and stitch to top of head. Make tail by sewing a piece of string to top edge of base.

**This is the cat
That killed the rat . . .**

My cat is the finger of a glove, made just like the kittens on page 14 but I tied a bow of narrow ribbon round his neck. (Your cat could be white or grey, if you prefer.)

**This is the dog
That worried the cat . . .**

Prepare a body as given for father bear and mouse on page 83 making

the 'hand strips' white. Oversew the two neck edges together. Place on one side. Trace and cut out two white felt head pieces (pattern page 93) two black felt ears, two eyes and a nose tracing from page 94. Stick ears, eyes and nose to one head piece. Draw in black hairs with felt pen. Embroider a white highlight on eyes. Stick the face to other head piece all round edges only, pushing a little stuffing inside as you work. Sew back of head to top of body. Give him a small ribbon scarf.

**This is the cow with the crumpled horn,
That tossed the dog . . .**

I also dressed up my cow just for fun (see plate opposite page 32). To make one like her, prepare a body complete with apron as given for mother bear and mouse on page 82 but insert hoofs cut from black felt into ends of sleeves. Oversew two neck edges together. Place on one side. Cut two whole head shapes in brown felt, tracing from page 94, and on one piece stick a white nose and black nostrils. Trace and cut out white felt eyes, black pupils and horns from white postcard taking the shapes from page 94 (remember to make one horn crumpled). Trace and cut out 2 brown and 2 white felt ears. Stick them together in pairs, fold base inwards and stick. Stick all these pieces in place. Stick the face to other head piece all round the edges only—pushing a

little stuffing inside as you work.
Sew back of head to top of body
(a little on one side?). Sew a little
lace frill round the neck if you wish.

This is the maiden all forlorn
That milked the cow with the
crumpled horn . . .

I made my maiden exactly like
Thumbelina on page 88 but gave
her a cotton dress instead of lace.
You might prefer to knit yours—
there are many ideas in other parts
of the book.

This is the man all tattered and torn,
That kissed the maiden all forlorn . . .

I made the man from the instructions
given for the clown on page 69
using drab coloured material for his
body and a piece of ribbon with
frayed ends for his scarf. I turned
the ends of his mouth downwards
to make him look miserable and
sewed a bundle of straggling,
uneven wool to his head for hair.

This is the priest all shaven and
shorn,
That married the man all tattered
and torn . . .

As you can see, I used the vicar
from the wedding group on page 22.

This is the cock that crowed in the
morn,
That waked the priest all shaven
and shorn . . .

I knitted my cock from the

instructions given on page 58 for a
rooster, using white wool with gay
feathers—however you could equally
well use black or brown for the
main colour.

This is the farmer sowing his corn,
That kept the cock that crowed in
the morn . . .

The farmer was made from the
instructions given for the clown on
page 69. I used a drab coloured
material for his body and gave him
a scarf of braid trimming. His hair
was four white bobbles stuck in
place like the father of the glove
family on page 11 and I gave him a
smiling mouth. I made his cap
from two felt circles oversewn
together and added a tiny peak
stuck to the wrong side, then stuck
the whole thing firmly to his head.

. . . That waked the priest all
shaven and shorn,
That married the man all tattered
and torn,
That kissed the maiden all forlorn,
That milked the cow with the
crumpled horn,
That tossed the dog,
That worried the cat,
That killed the rat,
That ate the malt,
That lay in the house that Jack
built.

Jack is knitted just like the sailor
on page 64 but I divided his body
into two for a jersey and trousers
and gave him a braid scarf.

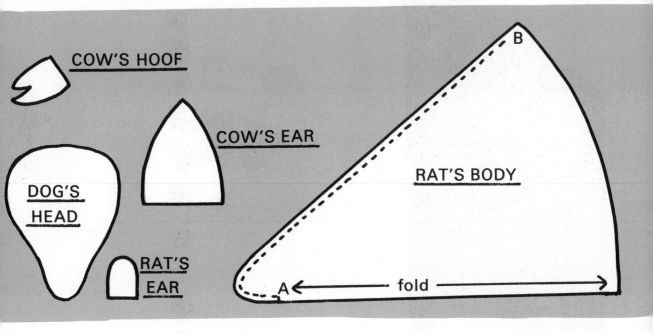

COW'S HOOF

COW'S EAR

DOG'S HEAD

RAT'S EAR

RAT'S BODY

B

A ← fold →

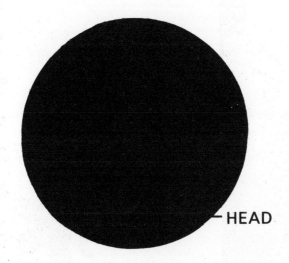

HEAD

MAN

PRIEST

FARMER

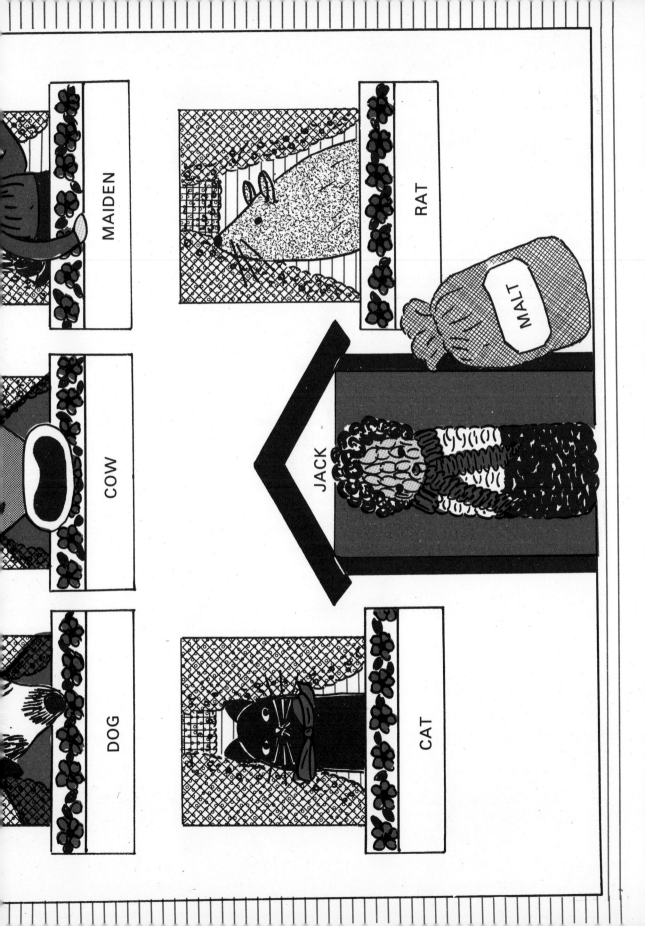

Goodbye

One hand makes the rocking, rolling sea,
And a glove with no thumb makes a boat for me!

I used parts of the designs of two of the puppets to make 'me' saying goodbye. Why don't you try altering and interchanging one with another? In this way you'll create lots of new and interesting characters.

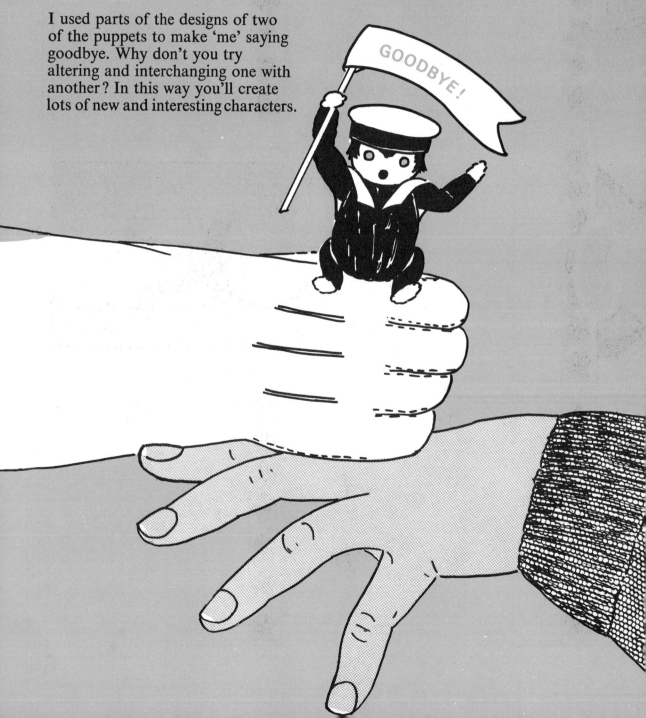